OPEN SEASON

True Stories of the Maine Warden Service

DAREN WORCESTER

Down East Books

Published by Down East Books
An imprint of Globe Pequot

Distributed by NATIONAL BOOK NETWORK

British Library Cataloguing in Publication Information available

Library of Congress Cataloging-in-Publication Data available

ISBN 978-1-60893-647-2 (pbk.)
ISBN 978-1-60893-648-9 (e-book)

♾™ The paper used in this publication meets the minimum requirements of American National Standard for Information Sciences—Permanence of Paper for Printed Library Materials, ANSI/NISO Z39.48-1992.

Printed in the United States of America

To the men and women of the Maine Warden Service.

Thank you.

CONTENTS

ACKNOWLEDGMENTS

THANK YOU THE WARDENS WHO CONTRIBUTED THEIR EXPERIences to *Open Season*: Bill Allen, David Berry, Dennis McIntosh, Gary Dumond, Glynn Pratt, Jim Brown, John Ford, John Marsh, Martin Savage, Mike Joy, Nat Berry, and Russ Dyer. Extra thanks to Nat Berry, John Marsh, and Mike Pratt for introducing me to the contributing wardens. I'd also like to thank Linda (Belanger) Perkins, as well as the other wardens named in this book, for their correspondence.

More thanks to Laurie Holbrook for the proofreading and encouragement, Coach Kent for serving as a publishing cairn, and to Michael Steere and Stephanie Scott for their editorial guidance.

Most importantly, thank you to my family for their love and support—especially my wife, Frances, who has survived countless Saturday-morning trips to the grocery store with potty-training children to grant me with precious time to "work." I couldn't have done this without you.

Introduction

The cliché of sportsmen telling tall tales is as old and worn as a favorite pair of L.L. Bean boots. That said, we still love to hear these stories because a friend or family member's point of view gives life to the tales, but what is easily overlooked is there's often an untold perspective. For every campfire story about that whopper of a salmon grandpa caught, there's a warden who's quick to point out that Rapid River is fly-fishing only. And that trophy buck? Funny thing there, too. It turns out, spotlights aren't permitted as scopes, and, this might be nitpicking, but antlers don't grow from duct tape. As a lifelong outdoorsman, I'm clearly toeing a fine line between good candor and heresy. You see, when we're talking about hunting down the truth in Maine's woods, we need to clarify whose version of the truth we're going with.

Call me crazy, but I tend to believe the storytellers who took an oath to perform their duties "honestly and faithfully." The others are just full of—well, you get the point. What you might not have known is that wardens can spin quite the unbelievable yarn themselves. This first dawned on me at my father-in-law Nathaniel (better known as Nat) Berry's retirement party. After thirty-four years of service, it was a fun-filled evening of conversations that began with "Remember that time. . . ."

The highlight of the night came when a warden named Chris Simmons stood before the gathering and cleared his throat. He was joined by Warden Tom Santaguida, and from the get-go, it was obvious their toast wouldn't be filled with undying praise for the man of the hour. The giveaway? They were giggling so much that neither of them could complete a sentence.

After taking a moment to collect themselves, Chris began, "Nat, you know we love you, but. . ." He went on to explain that working for Lieutenant Berry wasn't all fun and games. On the contrary, if they asked for time off to attend an event together, they were often told that coverage was needed, so only one of them could go. The choice of who was up to them, which, in effect, meant they didn't get to go.

One day, after missing out on an evening of carousing in Portland's Old Port, Chris received a nuisance wildlife complaint. A plump skunk with an appetite for trash had taken residence in a cul-de-sac community. Anyone who dared discourage the new neighbor quickly learned the hard way that it had no intention of moving out. Needless to say, this aspect of a warden's job can flat-out stink. Chris and Tom's moods were soured by the time they had caught the skunk and returned peace and aroma to the neighborhood. They came to the conclusion that the safest place to release the animal was into the wild of Lieutenant Berry's dooryard. Quite proud of themselves, it wasn't long before "coverage" was again needed during a bachelor party of a mutual friend, whereupon they figured one animal wasn't enough for a repeat offender.

"That was worth two skunks and a beaver," Tom declared.

Set back from the road and surrounded by forest and a small duck pond, Nat's backyard was an ideal place for animal relocation. Or so they continued to tell themselves.

By the third violation, they'd established a scorecard. This mischievous judicial system served its purpose for a couple of years, until the infractions were so numerous (or, perhaps, the judges had become too indiscriminate) that all nuisance wildlife was being released on Nat's property. On one occasion, they'd gone so far as to deposit a raccoon directly into Nat's new garage.

"Don't worry," Chris said. "We closed the door behind us."

"You didn't?" Nat shouted.

"Oh, we did. We kept a tally, and I have the list right here." Chris pulled a piece of folded-up notebook paper from his pocket and made a show of opening it. "At the top of our catch-and-release list are twenty-eight skunks."

Tom read the next one. "Twenty-five raccoons."

And so on down the list of problem critters they went, until . . . "Two opossums," Tom said, setting off another round of giggling. For a second, I thought this was the end, but then Chris raised his hand to say there was more. The room went silent.

"And one . . ." Chris said, pausing for dramatic effect, "black bear."

The resulting ovation was interrupted by the fire alarm—the timing of which was highly questionable, to say the least. As the crowd shuffled out to the parking lot, the only person not in stitches was my mother-in-law (go figure, she being the one who was home alone with the girls while her husband was out on all-night poacher vigils).

For me, this was the moment the seeds for *Open Season* took root. I didn't know it at the time, but many of the men in attendance that night would contribute to these twenty stories from twelve game wardens. Altogether, their cumulative experience represents more than three hundred years of Maine Warden Service folklore. With all due respect to Mike Joy—who is still an active-duty warden at the time of writing, and whose story of being stranded on a Sebago Lake ice floe was too unbelievable to pass up over an age requirement—all other stories are from retired wardens.

Before reality TV, GPS devices, and dashboard computers, these wardens presided over a coming-of-age era for the Maine Warden Service. It was a time when a compass, map, and their wits were what mattered most in the field. Every day offered the potential for an exciting new adventure, many of which endangered the wardens themselves.

As you read these stories, imagine yourself sitting around a crackling campfire. You might even have a cold beverage in hand. A man dressed in a flannel shirt and dirty work jeans sits on a log across from you. He's telling warden stories, and the weathered crows' feet around his eyes serve as proof of authenticity. Through the flames, you envision the man's younger self, clad in a warden uniform. Just remember that many of his stories take place before the Warden Service adopted the iconic green outfits we see today, and so he would have been wearing the same blue that's associated with the U.S. Air Force.

The man isn't just telling warden stories; he's sharing his life experiences. Through his eyes, we see what it was like to become a warden in 1960, banished to the far outreaches of Maine at a time when being handed a badge, service revolver, and law book, along with a hearty slap on the back, served as on the job training. His memory contains details of the Ludger Belanger disappearance that were never made public, and are enough to make any honest person's blood boil. The man speaking has been part of numerous daring rescues, at one time found himself needing aid after driving a snowmobile through lake ice, and has even been attacked by an enraged man with a chainsaw.

Not all of his stories are a matter of life and death. You hardly notice the fire dying down as he tells humorous tales of poachers being caught in compromising situations, lucky breaks in bizarre cases, and how trickery was sometimes their best approach. But before you get any grandiose ideas, know that being a warden isn't easy. In the fall, especially, it means endless days and nights away from family. This is trying for everyone, especially spouses, and you wouldn't be human if sometimes, amidst the doldrums of another all-night stakeout, you didn't wonder if it was all worth it. The answer is yes, of course—he wouldn't trade his career for anything, but you best know what you're getting yourself into.

He drops his head and there's a long moment of silence. The fire is nothing more than glowing embers now, and in the waning light you can hardly see his eyes as he asks if you really want to know what it was like to walk in his shoes? Because if you do, there's something else you need to know. Not all of his stories have a happy ending. His voice cracks as he speaks of a boy who slipped through river ice. It has been twenty years and he still thinks of the boy, sometimes unable to sleep at night. Are you listening? This is important. As vast and wonderful as the Maine wilderness is, there are inherent dangers. There's no group more skilled at outdoor search and rescue than the Maine Warden Service—you better believe that—but still, they aren't always able to save the day.

The man takes a deep breath and stokes the embers of the fire again. All of which brings us back to point of view. Believe it or not, the key aspects and incredible twists of these stories are all factual. Please bear in mind that some of these tales are over fifty years old, and the fog of memory can only go so far regarding exact conversations and environmental conditions. Creativity filled the gaps, and in these cases, my re-creations have been given the consent of the warden as being true to the spirit of the experience. Of course, many names and personal descriptions have also been altered to respect the privacy of those who, shall we say, might have a different campfire version of these stories.

Enjoy.

Chapter One

Welcome to the Maine Warden Service

Russ Dyer sat alone before a panel of four interviewers. Having already passed the written exam, his acceptance as a temporary Maine warden was in the hands of these men. Russ was sweating, no doubt through his rarely-worn dress shirt. The sweat was as much a product of the cramped, stuffy Statehouse room as it was the rapid-fire questioning. The interviewers took turns testing his knowledge of game laws as well as his mettle under pressure. He seemed to be handling himself well, even if the names and ranks of his questioners had already slipped his mind.

Except for one.

Maynard Marsh cleared his throat and took aim. "Alright," he said, looking more through Russ than at him, "let's say you're checking a brook for fishermen. You come across a woman fishing who's obviously very pregnant, and when you ask to see her license, she doesn't have one. What do *you* do?"

Russ hesitated.

His interest in becoming a warden was piqued by his job at L.L. Bean. Though he worked primarily with sewing tread onto boots, most of Bean's employees in 1960 were jacks of all trades, and it wasn't uncommon for Russ to find himself in sales, where he often interacted with retired warden Howard Wilson. For all the wild stories of northern Maine that Howard had told him, Russ couldn't recall any with a pregnant woman.

"I guess I'd probably issue a summons," Russ finally said.

"You'd issue a summons? You guess?"

"Yes . . . sir. She's fishing without a license. I can't see what the pregnancy has got to do with it—that's not my fault."

"You hope it isn't." If Maynard was joking, he didn't let on. "What do you think, young fella? What's the judge going to say when a big strapping game warden such as yourself drags this poor pregnant lady into court?"

He'd blown the question, Russ was sure of it, but he also knew to stick to his guns. "I can't see what the pregnancy has got to do with it. Why is she any different than the woman who's not pregnant?"

Aside from a *humph*, Maynard didn't respond. To this day, Russ doesn't know if he'd answered the question correctly.

He must have made a positive impression though, for shortly after that he found himself working a Durham field with Clement Baker. Clem had parked his warden vehicle, a '59 Ford sedan, in the back corner of the field where the tree line obscured it from the moonlight. Russ sat in the passenger seat, clad in a blue wool warden uniform with a new summons book in his pocket and a service pistol holstered on his side—all of which his temporary status required him to return after each assignment.

In the short time Russ had spent with Clem, he'd gotten to know him as a good-natured guy with a bit of a stutter, especially when excited. This mostly came across while they sat around waiting and Clem got worked up telling warden stories—something they'd been doing for a couple hours on one occasion when a car's headlights flowed across the field. It's illegal to light a field at night, even if shots aren't fired, so while the perpetrators returned to the road empty-handed, Clem was in pursuit. They caught up to the car about a mile down the road and pulled it over. There were two suspects inside; Clem approached the driver's door while Russ covered the passenger. Clem rapped on the window and politely asked the driver to open the door. Neither man inside the vehicle responded. They stared straight ahead with blank expressions on their faces, ignoring the wardens altogether.

Clem tried the door himself but it was locked. "I'm a game warden," he said more forcefully, "and I'm ordering you to o-o-open the door."

The men remained obstinate.

"O-O-Open the d-door!"

At about six feet, six inches tall, Clem was already an intimidating physical presence. Each time the men ignored his request it further stoked the flames of his frustration. Fortunately, after a couple minutes of this charade, the men must have realized it was in their best interest to listen. As soon as the driver unlocked his door, Clem ripped it open so hard the hinges broke. Clem then grabbed the man by his shirt, pulled him out of the car, and lifted him to eye level.

"When a G-G-G-God damn g-g-game warden tells you to o-o-open the d-door you better d-do it!"

The man nodded in agreement, his wide eyes looking for the ground as though he were afraid of heights—and Clem.

⚊ ⚊

The memory of Clem berating the man was still fresh in Russ's mind several months later, in the spring of 1961, when Chief Warden Elmer Ingraham invited Russ into his office. Elmer started the conversation by asking Russ about his experiences thus far with the service and whether he'd enjoyed it, before cutting to the chase:

"We have a full-time opening up north in Saint-Pamphile; are you interested?"

Russ already knew he had his wife's support. "Take what you can get," Carole had told him.

"Yes, of course," Russ said to Elmer.

"Good." Elmer shuffled several papers on his desk. "Could you start June 18?"

"I don't see how that would be a problem."

"Excellent." Elmer went on to explain there was a warden house in Saint-Pamphile that Russ and his family would be living in, and that he'd be reporting to Curtis Cooper, before asking: "Do you have any questions?"

"Yeah. Where's Saint-Pamphile?"

"You'll take the district and you don't know where it is?"

"Yes."

"Yesssss," Elmer said with the knowing air of a man who once sat on Russ's side of the desk. Opportunities were limited, and stations were based on seniority, so they all knew it didn't behoove a new warden to be discriminating. Elmer stood up from his chair and turned to a map of Maine on the wall behind his desk. "Well, it's right up here." He pointed to the top left of the state, his finger pressed against the Canada border. "This doesn't change your answer, does it?"

"Not one bit," Russ said.

"Alright then," Elmer said, holding out his hand to shake. "Welcome to the Maine Warden Service."

In mid-June, Russ and Carole packed their boys—two-year-old Daniel, and three-month-old Randy—into the family's '57 Fiat for the 300-mile drive north. Fortunately, Carl Bean of L.L. Bean had been supportive of Russ's goal to become a warden, and he allowed Russ to use a company truck to transport their belongings. As the two-vehicle caravan pulled out of their residence in Freeport, Russ had no idea he was beginning a journey that would one day return him to the Chief Warden's office in Augusta, where it would become his job to exile new recruits to the farthest out-reaches of Maine. At the time, neither Russ nor Carole really knew what they were getting themselves into. To them, Saint-Pamphile was a pinpoint on the map, a destination that appeared in their mind's eye as an exotic wilderness locale.

The journey to Saint-Pamphile didn't go without a hitch. Two young children in the car more than doubled the necessary quota for pit stops, and somewhere along the way the Fiat's muffler was lost to the attrition of rough dirt roads. The roar of the exhaust kissed the peace of sleeping children goodbye, making everyone more than ready for a vacation from the vehicle by the time they reached their destination.

When they finally arrived, Saint-Pamphile looked deserted. No one was around to point them in the direction of the warden house. It was a Sunday afternoon and the customs office was also empty. Most everyone in the seven-house settlement on the Maine side had crossed the border for the day to attend church and see to their weekly chores. The few people they did encounter spoke only French. After knocking on doors and canvassing the community for what seemed like an eternity, they eventually stumbled upon someone coming back from Canada, who spoke enough English to direct them.

Their new home instantly dissolved any idyllic notions of living in the great north woods. Upon scrambling from the car, they were greeted by a swarm of black flies that sent everyone fleeing for the house. Inside, the eighteen-foot square structure didn't exactly exude roominess. The downstairs was one large room that served as the kitchen and primary living quarters, along with a small bathroom built as an addition to the house on one side, and a walk-in shed on the other. A steep staircase led to what was said to be two upstairs bedrooms, but was technically one room with a divider.

As Russ looked around the house, he felt as though he were once again standing before Maynard Marsh, awaiting the results of yet another test. This time, it was Carole's verdict that counted, and while she wasn't one to complain, her silence was a sure-fire sign she was less than thrilled. And who could blame her? The house had been built by wardens, intended for one warden, maybe two, at a time. It wasn't exactly a setup conducive to a family with two young children.

"Russ," Carole said, "where is all this sawdust coming from?"

At first, Russ didn't know what she talking about. Then he noticed the sawdust strewn across the wood-planked floor. "Most likely the walls. It's the insulation."

"How does it get from inside the walls to the floor?"

"I'm not sure you want the answer to that."

"Why not?"

"Mice, I suspect."

The humor of the situation wasn't lost upon Carole. "I suppose living here won't kill us."

"Probably not. We'll have to wait and see."

On the kitchen table, Russ found a note from the previous tenant, along with the warden's log books. The note informed Russ that his supervisor, Curtis Cooper, would be around in a few weeks to meet him. In the meantime, the log books, for all practical purposes, would serve as Russ's instruction manuals. Still a year from entering the warden academy, his only training to date was his short stint on temporary duty and what he gathered from reading the biannual law book.

Russ jumped into the job doing what he thought was right, and it wasn't long before his summons book began to fill up. His biggest challenge was the language barrier. The lines on the map indicated Russ was living and working in Maine, but his day-to-day interactions were deeply rooted in French-speaking Quebec. Most of his work involved Canadian citizens illegally hunting in Maine.

On one memorable occasion, Russ and temporary warden Keith Gallant were driving along the international boundary in a department truck when they came across a fresh set of horse and wagon tracks crossing into Maine near Depot Lake. It wasn't long before they heard gunshots, and after a while, a farmer and his son of about twenty years of age came out with the wagon. They'd shot two deer on a Sunday in closed-season September. Russ asked them for a cash bond of $200, as well as to sign a personal recognizance, an agreement to appear in court at a later date that was standard practice when fifty miles or more from a courthouse. The farmer shook his head and spoke with a fast French tongue. Whatever he was saying, it was clear to Russ his message wasn't being received.

"You have to pay two hundred dollars," Russ said, raising his voice, as if breaking the sound barrier would also crack the language barrier.

The farmer responded in kind, somehow speaking even faster. Once again, all Russ understood was, "Non."

Russ opened his wallet to mimic payment. "YOU. HAVE. TO. PAY. TWO. HUNDRED. DOLLARS."

The farmer held out his hand in acceptance of Russ's mock payment.

Russ lost it. "If you don't pay, I'm going to burn the wagon and shoot the horse!"

"Non," the son said, stepping forward. He held up his hands in a sign of truce. "I'll get money."

"You speak English?" Russ asked.

"A little," the son said.

"Why didn't you say something before?"

The son shrugged his shoulders. "I'll get money."

Russ took a deep breath. He looked to Keith, who turned away from the scene and pretended to cough in a poor attempt to disguise his laughter, all of which made it hard for Russ to keep a straight face.

"That sounds like a good idea," Russ said.

An hour or so later, the son returned with a visiting doctor from Saint-Georges. The doctor paid the fine, explaining that he hired the farmer and his son to fetch some venison.

At the time, over-the-border venison trade was a common practice that kept Russ in business day and night, which made it all too apparent that the language barrier was going to make or break Russ as a warden. To avoid another situation like the one with the French-speaking farmer, Russ and Carole tapped into their Maine ingenuity. The following Sunday, Carole invited two women from the supermarket over for a regular game of cards. Hearts may have been what was dealt, but the opportunity to practice speaking French was the real game. Before long, Russ knew enough nouns to get his point across.

⸺ ⸺

The warden house turned out to be more hospitable than it first seemed, once they learned to let the shower run for a few minutes to allow the water to first freeze to the metal basin and then melt before getting in. Then there was the whole ordeal with the 300-gallon septic tank that wasn't draining until Russ bailed it out by hand. As far as the community was concerned, they were making friends. The local milkman, in particular, was a character unto himself. Speaking only French, and known to also peddle moonshine, he'd boast to anyone who'd listen about how smart the Dyer children were. The way he told it, the kids were only as tall as his thighs, and they could speak better English than him!

As time passed, Russ and Carole's wide eyes narrowed and Saint-Pamphile became a place they enjoyed calling home. Carole had been right—it didn't kill them.

Except, for Russ, the time it almost did.

He was sitting at the kitchen table, stirring his afternoon cup of coffee, his oldest son Daniel playing at his feet with wooden blocks when an airplane circled the house. This was the signal that someone wanted to see him. Russ threw on his coat and let Carole know he was going to the airfield, which, in Saint-Pamphile, was just that—a grassy field on the outskirts of town only big enough to land small aircraft. On this occasion, the thin snow crust crackled beneath Russ's feet as he approached the two men climbing out of the idling plane. Russ knew one of them, a local spray pilot named Joe Vienneau. The other man, who Joe introduced as Dan, was a sport from Connecticut. They'd been hunting out on Seven Islands and had shot two deer, and they wanted Russ to fly back to the island with Joe to tag them.

"What do you say?" Joe asked. "There's only room for two, so Dan's gonna take his stuff to the car and wait for us here."

Getting in Joe's plane had all the warning signs of a bad idea. It was a small, two-seat Cub that had seen better days, most evident by the thin telephone wire securing the struts.

"Well, you coming or not? I'm freezing my backside off out here."

As a young warden, Russ didn't want to admit he had reservations about getting in the plane. The spray pilots were an eccentric,

9

if not fearless, lot. Even back then it was fairly obvious the constant, close-quarters contact with pesticides wasn't doing the pilots any favors in the marbles department. At least Joe had a reputation for being on the respected, safe side of the fence, the telephone wire notwithstanding. All of which came down to one simple fact: If Russ didn't go, he'd never hear the end of it.

"I'm coming."

The plane rattled down the runway and slowly lifted into the air. The short flight to Seven Islands was mainly uneventful, except for the occasional jolt from a gust of wind. Inside, the cabin was an icebox from air seeping in around the doors and windows, adding to Russ's feeling of relief when they touched down with a thud in a field alongside the St. John River. A former farming settlement with around five hundred residents, Seven Islands was long since abandoned, the old buildings burned by the forestry department to dissuade vandals. Only a collection of foundations, fields, and forest ripe for hunting remained.

Joe led Russ from the plane to their campsite at the edge of the landing strip. A man dressed in a sheepskin coat—out of the ordinary, even for Saint-Pamphile—was sitting on a frozen deer carcass, heating a pot of tea with a blowtorch. With a mane of wild white hair that continued into a long, flowing beard and a bulky build, he looked every bit as though Santa had gone AWOL. Joe introduced the crazy-looking Claus as a fellow spray pilot named Merle.

"Mornin'," Merle said, despite it being mid-afternoon. He held the teapot up as an offer.

"No thanks," Russ said, convinced it was equal parts tea and milkman moonshine. The three men continued to talk, mostly about the deer, as Russ went about his business issuing the tags. Merle had shot the one he was sitting on, a six-point buck, and he didn't budge an inch while Russ reached around him to secure the tag. Adjacent to them was a slightly smaller four-pointer that was Dan's property.

"We better head back, eh?" Joe said once the tags were issued, "Dan's waiting and he's got a long drive ahead."

"I'll fly," Merle said, standing up for the first time since Russ's arrival. It took him a step or two to collect his balance.

"You sure?" Joe was the one to ask, but Russ was thinking it—mentally pleading, actually.

"Yep." Merle dropped his drawers and relieved himself in the middle of camp. "It's my turn."

"Suit yourself." Joe looked to Russ. "Mind grabbing an antler and help get this critter to the plane?"

The deer, likely no more than 140 pounds before it was field dressed, was an easy drag between the two of them.

"I have to ask," Russ said once they were out of earshot from Merle, "is he really—"

"Santa Claus?" Joe interrupted. "It sure would explain a lot." Joe stopped dragging the deer. "Hey Merle!" he yelled. "Are you Saint Nick?"

"You better believe it!" Merle shot back as he adjusted his trousers. He grabbed his deer by the antlers and raised its head. "And this here's Comet."

Joe turned to Russ. "That answer your question?"

"No, is he drunk?"

"Oh. I suppose that would also explain a lot." Joe slapped Russ on the back. "Don't worry, Warden, Merle's always like this."

"Great."

It wasn't until they got to the plane that Russ realized something else didn't add up. The seats were situated one behind the other with little legroom. Nor were there any storage compartments large enough to fit the deer.

"Where are we putting this?" Russ wanted to know.

"About that," Joe said with the sly grin of a man caught trying to pull a fast one. "You'll have to hold it."

"Are you serious?"

Joe nodded.

"Why didn't you fly it back with Dan?"

"There wasn't room with all his gear. Not to mention he's a paying customer. Had to make sure his charter on Saint-Pamphile Air was complete with first-class comfort."

"You've gotta be kidding. I'm not holding the deer."

"Unless Prancer can still fly," Merle said, coming up behind them, "it sure as hell ain't gonna be on my lap." Merle slapped Russ on the back. "C'mon, Warden, be a sport. Hop in the sleigh. It'll all be over in a couple minutes."

Russ climbed into the plane's back seat, at the moment too peeved to be restrained by his reservations for flying with Merle. Getting the deer in was another story altogether. They tried this way and that. First the antlers got caught on the doorframe. Then a hoof was jammed. Profanity was aplenty. In English and French. Perhaps it was a slip, but the buck suddenly dropped onto Russ, its head lay across his shoulder with the cut-open chest cavity facing him. Fortunately, the deer was frozen solid so blood didn't pour out.

Once the door was closed and the engine roared to life, Russ fully felt the weight of the deer across his chest. He could barely move, or, for that matter, breathe. It didn't help that the plane was rattling over an endless procession of bumps as it took off down the field. The runway paralleled the St. John River for a short distance—too short for Russ's taste—before ending abruptly at a ledge on the river bank with a ten-foot drop. Working into a headwind, it didn't seem as though they were gaining enough speed to lift off. The closer they got to the drop-off, the more apparent this became. They weren't going to make it.

"Whoa!" Merle yelled, pulling back on the throttle at the last possible moment. Russ gasped under the weight of the deer pressing hard against him as the plane came to a sudden stop mere feet from the edge. "Close call. Let's try that again, eh?"

Again?

"Are you sure that's a good idea?"

Merle laughed. A loud, eerie, don't-worry-about-it laugh.

"There's only one way to find out."

Russ tried to lean forward, to voice his concerns, but he felt restrained. One of the deer's antlers had pierced the seat cushion, and it was now securing him in place. Unsure what to do, Russ sat there, silent. Before he knew it, the plane was once again bouncing down the runway. Were they going any faster? It was hard to say. But it still didn't seem fast enough. With the end of the field rapidly approaching, there was no doubt in Russ's mind they were going to crash.

He could only hope it wasn't too bad. Maybe they'd survive if the plane somehow got across the river and into the brush. So long as they didn't end up in the water. Trapped beneath the deer, he'd drown for sure. It would be hours before any emergency services could arrive, especially considering the area's first responder was usually him.

The plane reached the end of the runway and Russ closed his eyes, thinking only of his wife and kids. A sudden drop sucked the air from his lungs. All hell was about to break loose. When it didn't, Russ opened his eyes to see they were flying along the river, so close he couldn't fathom how the wheels hadn't caught water. Still well below the tree line with a stiff headwind, they were far from in the clear. As the plane gained airspeed and slowly climbed, the wind's invisible hand batted them around like a cat toying with its prey. Russ's legs were shaking uncontrollably. Whether from nerves or the cold, it was hard to say. Likely both. The frozen carcass on his lap certainly wasn't helping matters.

Their flight path continued along the river for several miles before finally gaining enough altitude to get above the trees and turn back to town. Only when the plane completed a rough landing on the Saint-Pamphile airfield did Russ finally feel safe. While waiting for someone to get the deer off him, he couldn't help but think that his first year with the Maine Warden Service had been one long test. From Maynard Marsh's inquisition to his trial as a temporary warden, adapting to a new job in an unfamiliar environment, learning a new language, and now the spray pilots pushing his limits—he'd survived it all. And to think, he still hadn't attended warden school. Russ could only imagine what the future held, but he had the comfort of knowing there was one lesson he'd learned from this ordeal: Under no circumstances would he ever fly with Merle again. Even if he really was Santa Claus.

Chapter Two

Four-Finger Pete and the
Pulp-Hook Poacher

A CAR PASSED WITHOUT ANY SIGN OF STOPPING.

"What are we doing here?" Gayland Bracket wanted to know.

Nathaniel Berry, better known as Nat, dusted off his red wool overcoat and got up from behind an oak tree. Nothing appeared to have changed at the house across the road. It was a one-level ranch with a light on in a back room and the curtains drawn open on the bay window in the front. They hadn't seen anyone in the house all night, and there were no cars in the driveway. If the place was suspicious, it was for its lack of suspicion only.

"You want me to answer that?" Nat said. He continued to scan the area around the house, the right side of which gave way to a tract of swale grass as tall as corn stalks. Beyond the grass was a dirt tote road that ran parallel to a horse pasture. It was one of those overcast nights when the moon went on sabbatical, and they couldn't see much in front of them, let alone down the tote road. The horse pasture existed to them only in the occasional sound of galloping hooves.

"Humor me," Gayland said.

"Well . . ." Nat began. It was mild for October with a strong wind, and he waited for the latest gust to finish rattling the branches overhead. "We're preserving and protecting Maine's wildlife. Didn't you read the service bylaws?"

"Don't get me started. The only thing we're preserving and protecting here are our odds of getting hemorrhoids. These boys are probably out tying one on as we speak. I'll tell you what—we've got a better chance of pinching someone tonight if we go knocking door to door."

"You're welcome to it," Nat said, "but the next house isn't for half a mile."

"You know what I mean. How many times have we worked these all-night, see-nothing cases?"

"Too many."

"Exactly. I can't remember the last time one paid off."

While it was fun to bust Gayland's chops, Nat understood his thinking. They wouldn't be wardens if they didn't love this part of the job, but the monotony of a nighttime stakeout left plenty of room for the mind to wander. On an uneventful night such as this, Nat couldn't help but yearn for what he was missing at home—dinner with the family, the bedtime routine with his two young girls, reading stories, and rubbing noses with goodnight kisses. As much as his wife supports him, he also knew being away at night was tiring for her. His daughters were great kids, but they were at that age where they had a knack for not going quietly into the night at bedtime. At least, this seemed to be the case on evenings he worked, which in hunting season, was almost every night. With each passing minute of inactivity, the guilt grew. No one would admit it, but the other guys felt it, too. In a way, they were playing poker amongst themselves, and nobody wanted to be the one to fold. It just so happened that on this evening, Gayland flinched first.

"Alright," Nat relented. "Let's call the truck and see what they say." He unclipped his two-way radio. "Anyone home at Uncle Henry's?"

Wardens Jim Brown and Dave Georgia were stationed in a department truck about a mile away. It was Dave that answered. "We're here. Anything happening?"

"Nobody's home at Grandma's house," Nat said. "It might be time to hang it up. What do you guys think?"

"Think? I can't think," Dave said, "I'm too busy suffocating. Someone stinks. Seriously, my nose hairs are singed, and I can't tell if the culprit is Jake or Jim."

"I'd bet both," Gayland said.

"That's a good bet," Jim admitted. "Beans and franks for dinner. Both of us."

"Oh jeez," Nat said. "Better you than us, Dave. I'm just surprised Jake let you in."

Jake was Jim's two-year-old Chesapeake Bay retriever, a playful dog that easily stood waist high and weighed a whopping 126 pounds. Despite his intimidating appearance, the only time Jake showed aggression was when he was alone in a vehicle—a lesson nearly every warden eventually learned the hard way. At the time, wardens were permitted to bring their own dogs along, and Jim had only owned Jake for a couple of weeks, so Jake hadn't undergone any department training yet.

"It took some coaxing," Dave said.

"So what's the story?" Nat asked. "Are we in or out?"

"I say we stay," Dave replied. "Uncle Henry said the cousins wanted to play cards at Grandma's tonight."

Dave was being careful not to reveal anything over the radio, but they knew what he meant. He'd received a tip that two moose had been killed in the woods behind the house earlier in the day. It was believed a group of men would be going back for the moose that night, because they wouldn't want the meat to spoil in the unseasonably warm weather. The informant claimed to be a relative of the shooter. Each of the wardens wondered whether it was a hoax, but the caller provided names and they all checked out.

"I asked what I was going to get for meat," the informant explained to the warden, "and they said 'Nothing—just get your ass over here and help!' So I figured I'd show them."

"I want to play cards, too," Gayland said, "but they may have already come and gone. Or maybe they're playing somewhere else, and the joke's on us."

"We didn't get here 'till 7:30," Gayland continued, "and we haven't seen their cars all night. It's getting close to midnight. At some point, we have to call it."

"Dave, it's your call," Nat said. Dave was the youngest and least experienced of the four district wardens, but it was his district they were in and thus his decision. The radios went quiet for several minutes, which probably meant Dave was talking it over with Jim.

The radios finally crackled. "Ten more minutes," Dave said, "then we'll come get you."

"Ten-four," Nat replied. "Over."

"Ten minutes," Gayland mumbled to himself.

Nat turned to Gayland, but he'd already wandered out of sight. He likely went up the road. In the distance, the horses were on the move again. Were they typically this fleeting? Or was something spooking them? It was easy to second-guess everything.

Something moved. Nat wasn't sure what he saw—if he saw anything at all. It was more of a feeling, his sudden shortness of breath and heightened awareness a signal that something wasn't right. He peered into the darkness, eyes drawn to the end of the tote road. At first, the road looked as vacant as it had all night, but then a figure emerged. All Nat could make out from the silhouette was that it was a person, but it wasn't Gayland. It couldn't have been; Nat would have seen him cross the road. His heart pounding, Nat adjusted his circular-brim service hat and started toward the figure. Whether or not the person saw Nat coming, the figure didn't move. It was just there. Maybe armed, maybe not. Nat tightly gripped his Kel-Lite flashlight in his left hand, ready to draw his pistol with his right hand if necessary. When he got within a couple feet of the figure, Nat switched on the light.

The figure, now a fully visible man, flinched and took a half step back.

"Good evening," Nat said. "What are you doing here?"

"Looking for my dog," the man said, his left cheek stuffed with chaw.

"Looking for your dog?"

"Yep." The man spat off to the side. Whatever he was doing, he'd worked up a sweat. Several clumps of dark, wavy hair were matted to his forehead. He kept glancing back and forth between the house and Nat, almost as if he was, in fact, looking for a dog.

"Where's your flashlight?" Nat asked.

"I don't have one," the man said. His hands were tucked into the front pockets of his dark blue hoodie sweatshirt and he showed no intention of removing them.

"What's this?" Gayland asked, his sudden appearance causing the man to flinch again. Gayland reached to the man's side and pulled his sweatshirt up, exposing an empty knife sheath. "Where's your knife?"

The man shrugged. "Must have lost it."

"Let me see your hands," Gayland said.

The man removed his hands from his sweatshirt pockets and held them out. He was missing multiple fingers on each hand, and he couldn't have had more than four total. More importantly, there was no sign of blood. Nat shined the light onto the man's blue jeans. Still no blood, but there were dark hairs all over him.

"Those wouldn't happen to be moose hair, would they?" Nat asked.

"Must be from my dog."

"You don't say."

"I think you've found our crow," Gayland said to Nat.

"What's a crow?" the man asked.

Gayland smiled. "It's you. The lookout."

The man spat again. "I'm looking for my dog."

"Looking for your dog with no flashlight?" Gayland said. "What's your name?"

"Pete."

Nat could hear something in the distance, a faint scraping sound. "Stay with Pete," he said to Gayland, before turning off his flashlight and venturing down the road. A little further along and around a bend, he encountered another dark figure. It was crouched low, moving slowly, and breathing heavy. Nat got within several feet and turned on his light. Before him was a man laboring like a plow horse. Unlike Pete, this man didn't startle at the sudden light. His head was down and a Yankees cap shielded his eyes. With a pulp hook in each hand, he was dragging two moose hindquarters behind him.

"For fuck's sakes," the man said. "Gimme a hand, will ya?"

"I don't think so," Nat said.

The man stopped dead in his tracks and lifted his head. "Ah shit, it's the fuckin' warden."

"Yours truly."

"What have you got here?" asked a voice from behind. Nat turned and the light from his flashlight reflected off the badges on Jim and Dave's hats.

"Where are the rest of you?" Nat said to the pulp-hook poacher. As soon as he did, there was a splashing sound in the swale grass. The tops of the stalks were swaying where a third suspect was making his way.

Nat took a step back but something caught him behind the knees and he fell. Before he knew what happened, Jake's wet nose was buried in his ear. Nat rolled over and collected his flashlight as he got to his feet. The light had gone out, but a quick knock in the hand corrected the problem.

"Jim," Nat said, "we've got to get him before he gets in the house." If they didn't catch the man outside, any evidence they'd have against him would be circumstantial. He could easily claim to have been in the house all night sleeping and there wouldn't be much they could do to dispute it. Nat ran down the road in hopes of cutting the man off. He faintly heard Jim tell Dave to stay with the pulp-hook poacher, his hearing trained on the splashing in the swale grass. Was Nat ahead or behind the man? He couldn't tell.

Nat reached the end of the road and turned onto the house's side lawn. A motion-sensor light came on. There weren't any tracks leading to the house, nor could he see where the man was in the swale grass. Another gust of wind swept through and swayed the stalks. Nat shined his light into the grass and pushed his way in. The spongy ground squished and sucked with each step. The deeper he went, the more everything looked the same, a maze of light and shadows. This was crazy. It could take all night to find the man in this mess.

The radio crackled and Dave reported that he had the other two missing suspects in custody. Nat glanced back at the house. Jim was on the side lawn trying to restrain Jake on a leash, and by the looks of it, he was doing all he could to hold Jake back. The monster of a dog was lunging forward, each tug pulling Jim a step or two. Jake's teeth were out in a vicious snarl and slobber flew with each violent bark. It was a side of Jake they weren't accustomed to seeing outside of the truck. Because he was untrained, there was no telling what would happen if Jim let go, but it sure looked like Jake was going to rip someone apart. Nat started to worry that he might be it, and it occurred to him that if he was feeling this way, perhaps the suspect was, too.

"Jim," he yelled so that the man in hiding could hear him. "Send in the dog."

"Don't send the dog," the man immediately yelled back. Two hands appeared over the top of the grass. "I'm coming out."

Jim was laughing. "Don't worry," he said, "Jake's not in the truck."

CHAPTER THREE

Ice-Out

Maureen turned off the bathroom light and the pine-board flooring creaked as she made her way to bed. No sooner did she slide under the goose-down comforter than her tabby cat nestled onto the other half of the pillow. For a second, the cat's gentle purring sounded like a person.

"Ivy," she said to the cat, "are you talking to me?"

Then she heard it again—a muffled yelling.

"The wind is playing tricks on me."

Maureen closed her eyes, but she couldn't put the strange sound to rest. Perhaps it *was* a person. It just didn't make any sense. In the dead of winter, all the surrounding camps were boarded up. She was the only year-round resident on this side of Sebago Lake for several miles. No doubt her imagination was getting the best of her.

But what if?

"This is foolishness."

Maureen swung out of bed and shuffled into her slippers. Using a quilt as a makeshift robe, she went to the sliding glass door. She hadn't opened it all winter, so the door didn't exactly cooperate, but Maureen managed it ajar nevertheless. A light breeze greeted her as she stepped into the foot-deep snow on the second-story deck.

"Is that what I think it is?"

There was open water along the shore, and yet someone appeared to be waving a flashlight on the lake. This wasn't her imagination. The yelling was all too real. Multiple voices screamed for help.

— ～ —

The Joy family was settled in for the night at the Naples Warden Camp. The kids were fast asleep in the bedroom while Mike and his wife Leeann were on the pullout couch watching the Nagano Winter Olympics. Drifting in and out of consciousness, Mike was mostly out when the phone rang at a quarter to nine. It was his supervisor, Sergeant Albert St. Savior, calling to say several fishermen were stranded on a Sebago Lake ice floe. They didn't know how big the floe was, or how thick the ice, but they needed to rescue the fisherman before an overnight cold front endangered everyone. Albert had already contacted Bob Burnham, a private contractor who built and operated airboats, for his assistance. Mike agreed to meet Albert at the residence of the woman who called in the report.

"You'll be needing this," Mike said, handing the television remote to his wife.

"Not for long," she told him, "I'm half asleep already."

"You too, huh."

"Yeah." Leeann propped herself up. "Listen—dress warm."

"Don't I always?"

She flashed him a look that said, "Who do you think you're kidding?"

Sporting the build of a linebacker, Mike's interpretation of dressing warm differed a bit from that of his wife. In this case, it wasn't worth the discussion. It was unseasonably warm for February with the temperatures in the high thirties, but a cold front was coming. This call had the makings of a long night and the pending winds would surely be felt on the lake. So Mike pulled on his department issued snowmobile bibs and forest green parka over his warden uniform. He then laced up his black leather boots and wished his wife sweet dreams.

Albert was already at the woman's house where the 911 call was made when Mike arrived, along with fire departments from three towns, both on-duty personnel and a battalion of volunteers. Between the snowbanks and the influx of vehicles, it was tight maneuvering along the narrow lakeside road. Getting the airboat through there was going to be a feat unto itself. Mike parked at the beginning of the mess and walked in, the flashing red lights from the fire trucks flickering on everyone's faces as he approached the crowd. Introductions were self-serve, and Mike started with a few familiar faces. Many of the firemen were dressed in immersion survival suits. They looked more prepared for a moonwalk than anything else, the canary yellow suits covering them from head to toe, leaving only their faces exposed.

"The boat's here," someone announced before they could establish a plan, which set off a domino effect of vehicle moving and crowd clearing. It took a while, but once the airboat was in the water, Albert and Mike regrouped.

"Do you want to stay here to man the radio and coordinate everything?" Albert asked. "Or do you want to be in the boat?"

As a member of the Warden Service's search and rescue dive team, Mike's answer was a foregone conclusion. "The boat."

They made a quick rescue plan, which took into account the likelihood of making two trips. Bob strapped on his orange life preserver and took the elevated operator's seat. Mike and a firefighter named Liz also donned their life preservers and sat on lower pads to each side of Bob. The engine started and the propellers began to spin, the deafening noise soon extinguishing any conversation.

A gentle breeze cooled Mike's face as the boat picked up speed. Small, rippling waves were beginning to form on the lake, a sign the weather was changing. They traveled the distance of a football field before the ice sheet came into view. The floe was massive, stretching beyond what could be seen in the dark. Mike counted five fishermen awaiting their arrival as the airboat coasted in to avoid creating a wake. Bob nosed the boat about three-fourths of the way onto the ice.

Mike stood and held his hands in the air to the fishermen. "Stay there!"

Liz was first out of the boat to test the ice. Trained for cold-water rescue, she knew exactly what to do. "It's okay."

Wearing a shoulder harness affixed to a nylon rope, Liz proceeded to the bow where she tied the rope to the airboat. This tether would enable Mike to pull her back if she had to perform a water rescue. Once Liz was properly fastened, Mike handed her a spare lifejacket, and she walked out to the fishermen.

Mike stood next to the airboat watching as Liz explained the procedures to the fishermen. She put a life preserver on one of the men and led him back to the airboat. Mike helped the man in and gave Liz another life preserver. Without wasting a second, she was off on another retrieval. At this pace, Mike would be home and in bed by midnight.

The airboat's propellers were creating such a loud whooshing sound that when the second fisherman arrived at the boat, he had to lean into Mike and yell.

"Man, I've never been so happy to see a warden before."

Mike laughed. "If I only had a nickel." These guys knew they screwed up; there was no point scolding them now.

"I bet."

Mike held onto the fisherman as he stepped gingerly into the boat. The man merely had one foot in when a loud slapping sound at the back stole Mike's attention.

"What the—"

The propellers were hitting the water.

"We're sinking!" Bob shouted from his perch.

"Everyone out!" Still holding onto the second fisherman's arm, Mike yanked the man out. There was a cracking sound. Then a splash. Mike was suddenly standing in a foot of water. Their section of ice had broken off from the main floe, and the airboat was taking it under, the bow rising like a drawbridge. The first fisherman into the boat had little choice but to jump, landing near the top of the sinking ice. It wasn't enough. The man slid into the water, flailing and screaming for help. Liz immediately jumped in after him while the remaining fishermen on the main floe added to the chaotic shouting.

Mike was also in trouble, waist deep and slipping off the sinking ice. His snowmobile bibs offered little resistance to the winter water engulfing his legs. He grabbed the top edge of the sinking ice and fought to pull himself out of the water, but the weight of his soaked clothes and boots, along with his gun belt, radio, and Kel-Lite, made it a struggle.

"Grab my hand!" someone yelled.

Mike looked up to see the fisherman who'd been happy to see him reaching over the top of the ice. They locked arms and the fisherman strained to pull Mike up. They weren't getting far until someone else grabbed Mike by the armpits. Together they hoisted him over the top of the ice. The second person to help was Bob. Somehow he'd made it onto the floe without getting wet.

Not far away, two other fishermen helped Liz get their buddy out of the water.

Mike did a quick head count. Liz was still swimming, but everyone was safe for the moment.

"Unreal," one of the fishermen said, pointing to the boat.

The propeller's cage had just gone underwater. The airboat was completely vertical, its rear spotlights illuminating the water as the boat slipped into the abyss. The broken-off section of ice was also upright. Once it was free of the boat, the ice shot out of the water, washing a wave onto the main floe. For a moment everyone was silent, mesmerized by the blue, aquarium-like effect of the airboat's lights sinking out of sight.

"I'm tethered!" Liz yelled. "I'm tethered!" She pulled and jerked at her harness's karabiner, unable to free herself. What little remained of the nylon rope's slack was floating on the water, vanishing before their eyes. "Somebody help!"

"Does anyone have a knife?" Mike shouted. "We need a knife!"

A chorus of responses shot back. Most said no, but one of the fishermen unsheathed a buck knife and cut her free before the slack tightened.

"That was close," another said as they watched the rope disappear.

Mike assessed the group. The man who attempted to board the airboat second was wet to his waist, as was Mike. Then there was the guy who'd gone in. "What's your name?" Mike asked him.

"Kevin." His lips were blue, and he was already shaking.

"Do you have any other clothes?"

"No."

"Does anyone?"

"What I had was in the boat," Bob said.

"Me too," Liz replied.

There wasn't a "yes" amongst the fishermen.

Mike turned back to Kevin. "Take off your upper layers. You can wear my coat." Mike shed his jacket and handed it over, along with his insulated warden's ball cap. "Does anyone have a blanket or anything we can use to keep Kevin warm?"

"There's a canvas tarp covering the sled," one of the fishermen said. He was a toothpick of a man with a blonde beard down to his collar. He wore a beige Carhart parka and a hunter orange wool hat.

"What's your name?" Mike asked.

"Tom, but the guys call me Moony."

"Okay, Moony, get the tarp and wrap it around Kevin. I'm going to radio for help."

Moony unfastened the bungee cords holding down the tarp. The tote sled underneath was wooden and likely homemade. Its primary purpose, it appeared, was to transport their cooler. Mike needn't ask what was inside. No doubt it was a contributing factor to their current situation.

"Two-one-two-five to two-one-two-seven," Mike said into his portable radio, naming his and Albert's call numbers. "Do you copy?" The radio had gotten wet, and it was hard to say if it was even working. There was some static, but no response. He repeated the message several times without any luck. Then he tried calling the barracks. All eyes were on him now, the looks on everyone's faces saying it all.

"Don't worry," he said. "They know we're here. They'll come looking if they don't hear from us soon." Mike un-holstered his .357 Magnum. "Let's see if I can get their attention this way. Everyone stand back."

He fired three consecutive shots into the water. The wind was picking up, a steady flow whipping across the lake. Could they hear the shots on shore? The ice floe was drifting farther and farther away, the faint smattering of lights on the horizon no brighter than stars in the sky. If they could see the stars, that is. The cloud cover had created an empty darkness perpetuating their sense of isolation. Several long minutes of waiting returned no response. Mike fired another round, which also proved futile.

"Two-one-two-five to any law enforcement officer," he called into the radio. "I'm stranded on a Sebago Lake ice floe with seven others. We need immediate assistance."

Nothing.

He pounded the bottom of the radio with his palm as if to knock some sense into it and tried again.

And again.

Then the radio crackled. The signal was weak, the message intermittent.

". . .Cumberland County Sheriff . . ."

"Can you hear us?" Mike asked.

"Ten . . . notified dispatch . . . help is on the . . ."

Mike thanked the sheriff. "We're good," he said to the others, "Martha in dispatch will take care of us." His announcement set off a round of hoots and hollers.

"While we wait," Mike said after everyone quieted down, "how about someone tell me how we got here in the first place?"

Silence.

"C'mon guys, don't get shy on me now. I bet your wives wanted you out of the house, but this is a bit excessive—don't you think?"

Moony spoke up. "Believe it or not, Warden, but we walked out here."

"You walked?"

"Yep. We were going cusk fishing, you know. When we got down to the lake, there was a crack in the ice. Just a couple feet wide so we figured it'd be okay."

"Wait. This started as a crack?"

Mike looked toward shore. The rescue team's lights were even fainter than before.

"Yeah."

"We laid the sled across the crack and were able to get over it fine. Didn't think much of it. Walked out to where we could cast into open water. We were probably out here for a couple of hours before I noticed our lines drifting. There's no current here, so I knew something wasn't right. Told the boys to reel up. We were getting nervous and all, but it wasn't until we saw the open water between us and the shore that we realized we were fucked." He paused. "Sorry."

"It's okay. We're not in church."

"No, but we could use the guy upstairs right now."

"Nah, he can take the night off. We'll be fine—we've got Albert. There's a reason he's named St. Savior."

Mike turned his attention to Kevin. "How are you holding up?"

"Hanging in there."

"Keep moving. Keep the blood flowing. If you have any food, eat a little at a time. It'll help generate body heat." Mike turned from the group and dug his foot into the floe. The top layer was a honeycombed crust, light and flaky, which quickly gave way to a mess of slush. It was a good six inches before he hit solid ice. But how solid was the ice?

"Boat!" someone yelled.

Sure enough, two of the firemen had come out in a twelve-foot aluminum boat. With the increasing wind, the group hadn't heard the sound of the engine coming.

"Everyone stay put!" Mike shouted.

The fireman steering the boat nudged it sideways against the ice floe and killed the engine. "How do you want to do this?"

Mike thought about it for a moment. "How does the ice look?"

The fireman at the front of the boat chipped away at the ice with a paddle. "It's not great. Maybe two good inches at the edge."

"I don't know," Mike said, more to those around him than the firemen. These were the words they didn't want to hear. "It's just not safe. If the ice gives and you end up in the water, there'll be no way to get you in the boat."

"It's your call, Warden," Moony said.

Mike turned to the boat. "It's too risky. What's the backup plan?"

"There's talk of a helicopter," the fireman at the front of the boat said, "but let's get you connected with Albert." He held up a two-way radio for Mike to see. "Here, catch." Mike caught the radio like a football. He asked the fireman to round up dry clothes for those who'd gotten wet, and once they left Mike called Albert and updated him on the situation. In turn, Albert told him they were working on getting a helicopter out of Brunswick. At this point, it was an hour out.

"I don't know," Mike said. "I'm not sure the ice can take the rotor wash."

"We can always test it out further up the lake. I'll make some more calls to see if we can get another airboat. Just in case."

Mike didn't need to update everyone, they all overheard what was said. Bob, in particular, had a worried look about him.

"Don't worry," Mike said to Bob, in the process nudging him away from the group. "We'll get the dive team out here tomorrow to get the airboat back."

"Right now that's the least of my worries." Bob kicked at the crust below his feet. "I saw you checking the ice. What have we got? Three? Maybe four good inches?"

"About that."

"The wind is picking up."

"It is. Are you cold?"

"No, I'm fine, thanks. I have a hat and jacket. How are you holding up?"

"I'm good. Couldn't get cold if I tried."

"Waves are starting to form on the lake."

"They are."

"We both know what that means."

"We do."

"The wind is going to get stronger."

"It is."

"The waves will get bigger."

"They will."

"The ice won't hold up."

Mike smiled. "We have time."

"Not much. It's already after midnight. This cold front is going to hit us full force any minute now, and if those waves get going like we both know they will, this entire floe will be gone before dawn."

"Bob, we're going to be all right. Albert's working on it. We'll be out of here in no time, you just wait and see. Tomorrow night we'll be eating steaks. On you, of course."

"And what if they don't get the helicopter in time?"

"Then the steaks are on me."

"I'm serious."

"So am I. Just be patient. They'll get us. You do make a good point, though. We don't exactly know what condition this ice is in to begin with, and we can't be too careful." Mike turned back to the group. "Everyone, we need to spread out. Try to stay about ten feet apart from each other, except Liz should stay with Kevin. We need to balance our weight out."

"Hey!" one of the fishermen shouted as they moved apart. "I see something. Over there!" He was pointing across the floe. "It looks like an ice shack."

"I see it too," another agreed. "Let's check it out."

"Guys, wait," Mike said, but they kept going. "Stop!"

"Warden, we gotta see what's over there," said the man who first spotted the shack. "We don't know how big this floe is. What if we can walk right off it?"

"No. Nobody's going anywhere." Mike pointed to shore. "The lights are gone. We're completely disconnected and floating further and further onto the lake. There's no walking off."

"At least let us check out the ice shack. We could get Kevin out of the wind, and there might be a stove inside."

"I know, but where there's a shack there's also a hole in the ice. It's been too warm lately; we can't trust it."

"How about I check it out?" Liz said. "I don't mind going for another swim."

"That works. Everyone else stay here."

They all watched as Liz faded into the darkness. The further away she got, the more it looked like she was walking on the moon. While she was gone, the firemen returned with dry clothes. They were able to get both fishermen changed and wrapped in wool blankets. Mike got a new pair of snowmobile bibs, which he now wore without pants underneath.

"You were right about the ice shack," Liz said to Mike when she returned. "It's bobbing."

"Alright, thanks for checking." Mike turned to the others. "Sorry guys."

A disappointed silence fell over the group. "Figures," someone eventually said.

In search of good news, Mike called Albert. "What's the status on the helicopter?"

"It fell through. Don't worry, we've located another airboat, and it's on the way."

"ETA?"

"Soon. Hopefully no more than an hour. How's everyone holding up?"

"Getting restless. We have one high-risk for hypothermia, possibly two."

"Emergency services are here and ready to treat as soon as we get them to shore. Make sure they're on the first boat."

"Will do."

It was around one o'clock in the morning and time had flown up to this point. Now, seconds dragged into minutes, and each minute seemed an hour. The wind continued to pick up steam. Waves crested with white caps. The ice, moaning beneath their feet, was visibly deteriorating. Each wave splashed a little more away, often in sizable chunks. They moved the group further back. How was time both standing still and running out?

Mike's ears were stinging. The firemen had come and gone a couple more times, and somehow he kept forgetting to ask for a hat. He traded the radio from one hand to the other to alternate cupping his ears with his free hand. They were going to get off the ice safe and sound. He just knew it. There was no doubt the guys would get them. If only the others in the group were as optimistic. They were getting short with each other, their expressions flickering with fear. So Mike clung to the radio, listening to the back-and-forth amongst the wardens, waiting for good news to raise everyone's spirits.

"You're not going to believe this," Mike heard Warden Dennis McIntosh say to Albert on the radio. "The airboat hit a tree on the access road. It's stuck pretty good. Might take fifteen or twenty to get it out."

"Ten-four," Albert replied. Mike could only imagine what he was saying off-air.

"That don't sound good," Moony said, his mustache littered with icicles.

"It's not as bad as you think. Usually, when we're doing search and rescue, we have to find the missing people. In this case, they know exactly where we are. All they have to do is get the airboat out of the jam, and we'll be off this slab once and for all. They're really close."

"I s'pose."

"Trust me, we have time."

"Some of us more than others." Moony nodded to Kevin, who had Liz at his side.

Mike approached them both. "How's he doing?"

Kevin tried to answer for himself, his eyes dancing around the group as he searched for what to say. Visibly shaking, he formulated something, the only word of which Mike could understand was "cold."

Mike and Liz exchanged knowing looks. It didn't take training to know hypothermia was setting in.

"Do you guys have any soda in that cooler?" Liz asked the fishermen.

"What for?" Moony wanted to know.

"It'll help raise his blood sugar level."

"Nah, all we got is beer."

"That won't work."

"What about us?" One of the other fishermen asked.

"What about you?" Mike intervened.

"Can we drink the beer?"

"Seriously?"

"Yeah, man. I've got cotton mouth wicked bad. I need to drink something."

Mike shrugged. "Sure. Why not?" He watched as they handed out cans of Budweiser. Was this happening? A bunch of guys standing around drinking beer as if nothing was wrong. Did they even realize it was the beer that had gotten them in this predicament? Still, Mike wasn't going to deny them the pleasure. It could be their last.

"Hey, Warden," one of the men said. "You want one?"

"No thanks," though Mike did wish he had something non-alcoholic to drink. The constant wind had also dried out his mouth.

"You sure? I won't tell."

"I'm good."

As they continued to wait, the weather's gradual deterioration kicked into overdrive. Gale-force winds descended upon them as if they were standing in the back of a moving pickup truck. Mike turned away from the wind, his cheeks burning. All of which was little concern compared to the waves beating the ice. With each flush, they could feel the floe undulating beneath their feet. It was enough to make someone seasick.

A loud crack startled them all.

"Holy shit!" someone yelled.

About twenty yards away, a section of ice the size of a fire engine split from the main floe.

"Everyone back!" Mike shouted. Then, into the radio, "Albert, where's the airboat?"

"They're backing it into the lake now. Hang in there."

"Tell them not to drive the boat onto the ice. The floe's starting to break apart. Albert, we don't have time for two trips."

"What if we bring out the aluminum boat and park it next to the airboat?" Albert's voice was steady, as if this was a contingency plan he'd thought of hours before. "People can step from the airboat into the aluminum."

"That'll work."

"Great. Anything else?"

"Hurry."

The group was a sad sight to behold; everyone hunched with their backs to the wind. It would have been easier for them to stay warm if the ice could have supported them bunching like penguins. Instead, they settled for moving in place, though no one dared to run or jump or do anything that would stress the ice. They looked like a class of awkward middle school kids slow dancing to an unfamiliar song.

"Listen up," Mike shouted. "The airboat is on its way. When it gets here, Liz is going to escort us one at a time, starting with Kevin. Everyone else will get their turn based on proximity to the boat. I'll go last. The firefighters are also coming out in their boat so we can do this all in one trip. A few of you will have to climb from the airboat into the firefighters' boat. Any questions?"

Another crack. This one broke at the edge of their group.

"Back!" Nobody had to be told twice. They quickly moved away from the water. Mike didn't know how much longer the floe would last. Minutes? Seconds? He'd never watched lake ice go out, but there was no doubt that this was it. Floating chunks of ice filled the water around them, and more broke away with each jabbing wave. Maybe Moony was right about the guy upstairs.

Someone yelled, and Mike turned around to see the airboat magically appear at the edge of the ice floe.

"Let's go!"

Liz ushered Kevin to the boat and hurried back. It was a stark contrast to the orderly escort she conducted the first time around.

The ice continued to boom and crack around them but nobody panicked. One by one, Liz brought them to safety.

"Get me in that boat and steaks are on me," Mike said when Liz came for him. He put on his life preserver. "Just don't tell Bob." They were halfway to the airboat when the ice cracked beneath them. "Run!" Mike could feel the ice giving way with each step and the water splashing behind him. He crashed into the boat, sucking for air.

No one said a word. They all stared in disbelief at the chunks of ice drifting apart, knowing they'd been seconds away from going in the water. The next thing Mike knew they were on shore among the flashing emergency lights. A crowd of people hurried about in a state of controlled chaos. Mike stood watch as several EMTs loaded Kevin into an ambulance. Then someone grabbed him by the arm and ushered him into one.

It was Albert. "What the hell happened with the boat out there?"

"I don't know. We were loading people in fine, and then the next thing I knew it was taking on water."

"I'm glad you're okay." Albert handed him the ambulance phone. "We can talk later. You better call your wife now."

"Why? Have you talked to her?"

"No, but didn't you see the news trucks out there?"

Mike shook his head.

"This ordeal has been all over the news for several hours now. I'm sure Leeann is worried sick."

Mike called. His wife sounded half asleep when she answered.

"Don't worry," he said, "I'm fine."

"What? Why? What's going on?"

"I'm sorry. I didn't mean to wake you. I thought you knew. Albert said it was all over the news."

"What's all over the news?"

"It's nothing. Go back to bed, I'll tell you in the morning."

Mike could hear his wife turn on the television.

"Oh my God . . . oh my God . . ."

"Leeann, it's fine. It's all over now."

"Where are you?"

"In an ambulance." He immediately wished he hadn't said that.

"What?"

"Don't worry, it's just precautionary."

"There's nothing precautionary about an ambulance."

"Leeann. I'm fine."

"This doesn't look fine. You could have hypothermia."

"I don't."

"How do you know?"

"Because I took your advice. I dressed warm."

Chapter Four

The Unfrozen

"Yep," the clerk at the Bowdoin Town Store said, diverting his attention from the Bruins game on a small, black-and-white countertop television. He was an older gentleman, likely pushing his late sixties, who didn't appear the least bit uncomfortable to be sitting on a wooden stool. "Mitch was here—five, maybe six hours ago. Bought a twelve-pack of Coors. If you ask me, he could have done without it."

"Why's that?" Warden Bill Allen wanted to know. He had the build and determination of a bulldog, and at five feet, nine inches tall, he was still looking eye to eye with the seated clerk.

"I'd bet the store he'd been hittin' the sauce already. He came in on a sled but he wasn't wearing a coat or ski pants. Not even a hat. Don't know anyone in their right mind that'd be out on a day like this dressed like that." The clerk crossed his arms, "Damned near suicide."

Bill gave a knowing nod. Whether the old-timer realized it or not, from what Bill knew of the missing person, he'd fallen on tough times, and the clerk may have just hit the nail on the head.

"Why'd you sell to him?"

The clerk furrowed his bushy gray eyebrows. Bill was almost fifty years old, but the clerk was looking at him like he was a kid that'd stolen a candy bar.

"Do I look like his mother?"

Bill took a sip of coffee to swallow what he wanted to say before responding. "You remember what Mitch was wearing?"

"Just his blue work jumpsuit. He's a mechanic."

"Do me a favor," Bill said. "If anyone comes in on a snowmobile tonight, ask if they've seen Mitch or his yellow Ski-Doo." Bill wrote the number for dispatch on a piece of scrap paper and slid it across the counter. "If you hear anything, call this number."

"Will do. I hope you find him. He's not always on the straight and narrow, but he's a good kid."

"I hope so, too. Stay warm." Bill put a dollar on the counter to pay for the coffees and stepped outside. A gust of wind nearly ripped the door off the hinges. The cold air on Bill's neck sent a shiver down his body. The temperature was a blistering minus ten without factoring wind chill. If it was true that Mitch wasn't wearing any winter clothes, this wasn't going to be a pretty situation. Six hours were a damned long time to be snowmobiling in weather like this without proper clothing.

Bill returned to the warmth of his idling department truck, where Warden Doug Kulis was in the passenger seat surveying the DeLorme map.

"This is for you," Bill said, placing Doug's coffee on the dashboard.

"Thanks," Doug said. He pointed to Route 125 on the map. "We're here, not far from the intersection with 201. No surprise, there's trails everywhere 'round here. Mitch wasn't the last one to come through, but he's riding an Elan Ski-Doo, so I might be able to follow his narrow tracks." Doug drew a large circle with his finger around their location on the map. "You can take the truck and patrol these side roads."

Together they unloaded the department's long-track Arctic Cat snowmobile from the trailer. It took several pulls for the engine to sputter to life. After letting it idle for a moment, Doug gunned the throttle and snow shot from the track as he drove the sled over the giant parking-lot snowbank and down the trail.

Bill climbed back into his truck, cradled his coffee cup between his legs, and drove north on Route 201. He turned onto a side road that paralleled a field. The truck was immediately blasted by wind. Bill gripped the wheel tightly with both hands to steady the vehicle and swore as coffee spilled onto his leg. Snow was swirling around the truck and he couldn't see a thing out the windows. He brought the truck to a stop as the wind continued to shake the vehicle.

"This is nuts," Bill said to himself. If he couldn't see anything out his windows, he could only imagine how Doug was faring on the sled. In all likelihood, the blowing snow was erasing any sign of Mitch's snowmobile tracks, and perhaps the trail altogether. If by some miracle they were to find Mitch in these conditions, he was probably already dead. Drunk and working on getting drunker, his survival instincts would have shorted a fuse. Then again, there was the question as to whether or not that was his intent. It was challenging enough to save someone who wanted to live in these conditions. Once they tossed in the towel—impossible. No doubt, Mitch was beyond the wardens' jurisdiction. This was priest territory.

That wouldn't stop them from looking. Bill and Doug would go all night if they had to, and come morning they'd request a full search for what would certainly be a recovery situation.

The whiteout around Bill's truck cleared. He took a long sip of coffee—he was going to need it—and drove ahead. It wasn't snowing, but the roads required plowing, drifts stretching to the centerline. He drove slow, watching the snow squalls dance across the road. His purpose was to scan the roadside for any sign of someone crossing, but unless they'd done so in the last fifteen minutes, it was fruitless.

Doug called to Bill on the radio.

"I'm here," Bill said, expecting Doug to echo a similar frustration.

"I've got the guy."

"Come again?"

"I've got the guy, his pulse is weak," Doug repeated.

"Where are you?"

"In a pine grove just north of Bradley Pond and about a mile from the trail crossing on Meadow Road."

Bill placed the call for emergency services and stepped on the gas. Upon locating the Meadow Road crossing, he hiked in on the semi-packed snowmobile trail until he found Doug's sled. There was a single track leading off the trail where Mitch had tried to drive out of sight. He'd then lain under a pine tree as if he was going to sleep. Mitch looked that way now, wrapped in the wool blanket Doug put around him—quite possibly too little, too late—his eyes closed and face washed of color, a tuft of black hair frozen to his forehead.

"He was unconscious when I got here," Doug explained. "Pulse is weak, hard to tell if he's breathing." He paused for a moment. "How the hell are we going to get him out?"

"The ambulance is on its way," Bill said.

"He doesn't have time for them to get in here."

"I know it."

The trail in had been rough going; it had the deeply grooved appearance of an old skidder path, and likely wasn't well traveled, which is probably why Mitch chose this destination. But maybe not. Bill shone his Kel-Lite through the pine trees in a circular pattern in case there was a cabin or a logger's warming shack nearby.

No such luck.

A gust of wind sprayed them with snow from the tree branches above.

"We'll have to meet the EMTs at the road. The snowmobile is our only option."

"We could sit him between us," Doug said, "but we'll have to unwrap his legs. He loses any more body heat and it will be the nail in his coffin."

Bill glanced down at Mitch, who looked to be about five feet, eight inches tall, maybe 155 pounds. "What if I lay on the back of the Arctic Cat and you put him on top of me? We can keep him fully wrapped this way, and if you go slow enough, I should be able to hold him."

"It's worth a shot. We don't have time for anything else."

Doug wrestled Mitch out of the snow while Bill laid on the sled, face up with his head at the rear. Mitch was lowered on top of him, and, taking a deep breath, Bill wrapped Mitch in a bear hug. Doug stepped onto the front of the snowmobile and Bill felt a jerk as it throttled forward. Mitch's body listed to the side. With his feet on the running boards, Bill squeezed the seat with his knees to keep them from tipping off. The snowmobile rocked and rolled over the trail's ruts and snow-covered debris. At several points they came precariously close to tipping. Bill continued to squeeze Mitch tight, his upper body leaning against the turns to keep from falling.

"Hang in there," Bill said to the frozen man on top of him, though it was more for his own benefit. It was only a mile to the road, but the terrain and the urgency of the situation made time stand still. Unable to do anything more than hold on, Bill focused on the dark silhouettes of the tree branches above. He knew they'd reached the road when the ambulance's flashing lights illuminated the trees. In no time at all Mitch was being lifted off Bill and onto a gurney, which was quickly transitioned to the ambulance. The EMTs checked his vitals and established he still had a pulse.

"Think he'll make it?" Doug asked as they watched the ambulance drive away to Parkview Hospital in Brunswick.

"He's alive right now. Hell of a job you did finding him."

"Thanks. Hell of a job you did holding on to him."

The two wardens went back to the store and parted ways with a handshake. It was closing in on midnight, but Bill wasn't quite ready to go home and retire to bed. Wide-awake from the coffee and riding an emotional high from having saved a life, he picked up a boxed dozen at Dunkin' Donuts and stopped at the barracks in Augusta to share his celebratory snack with the dispatch crew.

"I'm telling you, people don't survive in this weather." Bill was holding court before the dispatchers, standing with a coffee cup in one hand, half-eaten chocolate donut in the other. "It's cold enough to freeze your eyeballs, and this guy's out on a snowmobile for several hours without a snowsuit or hat. And by some miracle he still has a pulse when Doug finds him."

A call came through.

"It's Parkview hospital," Dean Gardner, one of the dispatchers, said to Bill. A longtime member of the night crew, Dean had been on the edge of his seat, joking with Bill as he recanted the rescue. There were only two reasons the hospital would be calling, and so all eyes were on Dean as he answered. Within seconds his voice turned somber.

"What is it?" Bill wanted to know.

Dean held up his hand.

"What is it?" Bill repeated when the call was over.

"I'm sorry," Dean said. "Mitch died."

"Shit."

Bill's thoughts immediately turned to what they could have done differently. Given the situation, it was remarkable how soon Doug was able to track Mitch down, and they got him out as quick as possible. The truth was there was nothing more they could have done. Call it a harsh reality, call it warden luck. It wasn't the first time they'd lost someone, nor would it be the last, but there was always a pit in Bill's stomach when this was the result.

The change of events also meant Bill had some calls to make. He first woke Garrett McPherson, the on-duty officer of the day (better known as the OD), and relayed the full story.

"Tough break," Garrett said. "It sounds like you did everything you could."

As soon as Bill hung up with Garrett, he called the attorney general and repeated the story. The attorney general was likewise sympathetic.

There was no point going home. Bill wouldn't be able to sleep, unable to take his mind off the case, or the report he'd need to file tomorrow. He also had no interest in going to his office and writing the report, so he settled his rump onto the corner of Dean's desk, content to chide him for being a Lakers fan.

"You do realize that Bird was ten times better than Magic?" Bill said, firing the first shot.

Another call was coming through.

Dean took the call. At first his side of the conversation consisted of "Yes," "Okay," "Uh-huh." But then, "Are you serious?" Dean looked at Bill with wide eyes.

"What?" Bill wanted to know.

Dean held up his hand.

"Tell me now," Bill said.

Dean pumped his hand in the air at Bill as he said to the caller, "How is that even possible?"

"You're killing me." Bill said.

"He's still here," Dean said. "I'll let him know."

"Let me know what?"

The call finally ended.

"You're not going to believe this," Dean said, "but Mitch came back to life."

"Are you serious?"

"Yeah. He's got a pulse, breathing, the whole works."

"Are you shittin' me? So help me God, you better not be shittin' me."

"I'm not. The woman I talked to said that when they brought him in he had no pulse, no vitals, nothing for forty-five minutes. He was dead. Absolutely gone. But they wrapped him in heated blankets and were able to get his temperature up enough to get him going again. She said it's a medical miracle. She's never seen anything like it."

"Son of a gun," Bill said. "Well, you'll have to excuse me, I've got some calls to make." He rang the OD again. "Garrett, you're not going to believe this. The guy has come back to life."

"Which guy?" Though he'd answered the phone, it was clear Garrett was still gathering his senses.

"The one that froze to death."

"He's alive?"

"Apparently so."

"Have you been drinking?"

"No."

"Are you sure?"

"Yes. I'm serious. It's a medical miracle."

"Bill, I'm too tired for this crap, you better not be screwing with me."

"I'm not. He's alive. I swear."

Bill then called the attorney general, who on the second go around thought he was being pranked and was far less understanding than Garrett. After hearing words he didn't think possible from a man of such high stature, Bill figured he'd better head home before Mitch died again.

But first he rang Doug to let him know. They agreed to meet in the morning at the hospital to get background information for their report.

The next morning Bill saw a ghost when they entered the hospital's front doors. Walking toward them was a scrawny man with scraggly black hair, dressed in jeans and a gray sweatshirt, accompanied by an older woman they assumed was his mother. Bill couldn't believe his eyes. Was Mitch really leaving the hospital already? He was literally dead less than twelve hours before.

"Hey," Bill said when the two parties reached each other in the hall. "Are you okay?"

For a moment Mitch appeared surprised by Bill's inquiry, and then a look of clarity came over him. "Are you the guys that saved me?"

"We are," Doug said.

"Jeez, I really appreciate it." Mitch extended his hand to the two wardens. "I can't thank you guys enough. The hospital, they've got me on a treatment plan, and I'll tell you one thing: booze killed me once, it's not gonna do it again."

CHAPTER FIVE

The Wild Man of Fourth Machias Lake

THE SNOWMOBILE LAUNCHED OFF A DRIFT AND LANDED HARD with a burst of powder shooting over the already cracked windshield. Buck Pelletier jammed the brakes and howled into the wind. He dusted the snow off his wool coat and smeared his runny nose on his forearm. Not that it did much good—his sparse beard was already a collection of icicles.

Damn, it was cold. Even for him. He massaged his hands within his gloves as squalls of snow danced across the lake and whipped his face. Buck couldn't remember a spell like this, at least not in December. For the past six days, they were lucky if the high temperature reached zero, not counting wind chill, and overnight lows were sinking into the negative twenties. To top it off, folks at the general store were saying the front would stick around for a few more days. If this were how the winter of 1978 was going to go, Buck would need more firewood.

Only a fool would be out on the lake in this mess, which is exactly why Buck was here. Trapping season was just around the corner, and the cold was keeping the competition away, giving Buck a prime opportunity to scout beaver activity at the outlet and pick the best spots for setting traps. Nobody knew the lake better than Buck, so this was almost an unfair advantage. As long as he didn't cut ice or leave markers, his preview was perfectly legal. Squinting into the wind to get his bearings, he could tell by the shoreline that he wasn't far from his buddy Tim's cabin, and the outlet was just a bit further along. He'd be there in no time at all, and he could stop at the cabin on the way back to warm up.

Buck pressed the throttle and the snowmobile listed forward. Out of the corner of his eye, something in the snow caught his attention. Were those tracks?

His eyes weren't playing tricks on him. There were tracks, visible in the col between two snowdrifts, and mostly windswept. The tracks were big enough to be from a person, but who would be crazy enough to walk across the lake in this?

Maybe a moose?

Now this was worth investigating—the beavers could wait. If a moose had gotten into trouble, he'd put it out of its misery and fill his freezer. He could already see the look of surprise on his girl-friend's face. They were young and money was tight, so it will be a party tonight! Buck turned the snowmobile and followed the tracks as best he could. It wasn't easy. There were large gaps where the trail disappeared in the snow, and the path was erratic at best, which was how a moose might cross the lake. But something wasn't adding up. The tracks seemed too close together for a moose, and every time they veered in a different direction, they always came back toward the cabin. This pattern made sense if it was someone seeking shelter because it was the only camp on this side of the lake. But where would a person have come from? The closest plowed road was seven miles away. Maybe someone's sled broke down?

Upon shore, the mystery was solved. Sheltered from the lake wind, the tracks near the camp were clearly from a person's boots. They led to a window where the screen had been cut open and pulled back, the inside frame knocked in. It was hard to say for sure, the footprints were all crisscrossing, but it looked like someone had come and gone a couple of times.

"Hello," Buck called through the open window. "Don't try to hide, I know you're in here. It's okay, come on out." There was no response, nor any sign of movement. He went around to the front porch, where the snow blown into the doorway was undisturbed. Whoever broke in was only using the window. Buck unlocked the door and let himself in. The missing window pane was on the floor, shattered glass scattered about. The cabinets above the sink were left open and cleaned of food. The adjacent liquor cabinet, on the other hand, was fully intact—as best as Buck could remember, that is. There weren't many valuables in the camp to begin with, but everything seemed to be in place. Aside from food, the only other thing missing was the box of matches above the stove. The wood-box, however, was full, just the way he had left it. Buck opened the stove and the ashes inside were as cold and lifeless as the freezing air permeating the cabin.

"Doesn't make sense," he muttered to himself. If someone was in trouble, why didn't they stay in the cabin and start a fire?

Buck went back outside and found a set of tracks heading down the shoreline. He'd only followed them for about thirty yards when he spotted a black garbage bag sticking out from behind a large pine tree. It took him a moment to realize exactly what he was looking at. Buck stopped dead in his tracks. This wasn't a discarded bag of trash; it was a person wearing a trash bag.

Warden Glynn Pratt listened to Buck's story. The area around Fourth Machias Lake was part of Garrett McPherson's district, and Glynn had only been a warden for a year at this time, but he still knew of Buck Pelletier. As did all the wardens who helped cover the area. For anyone who thought trappers were an endangered species, Buck was the golden child. He was young, in his early twenties, and already one of the best woodsmen in these parts. While his reputation preceded him, the wardens had never caught him on the wrong side of the law, nor did they have any real reason to believe Buck skirted it. But when he routinely turned in more pelts than the old-timers, it made a warden wonder.

"What did you do when you spotted the man?" Garrett asked.

"At first, nothing," Buck said.

The three of them, along with state trooper James Townsend, were standing in a rough circle outside the Pine Tree Store in Grand Lake Stream. The wind was blowing and the temperatures plummeting, so they were all bundled up. Everyone, except Buck. He'd left his hat and gloves in his truck and appeared no worse for it. His face was windswept from being on the lake and his rabid, wiry blond hair barely flinched in the wind. Glynn had gone inside to get coffee when he'd arrived, and an old man sitting on the store's infamous liar's bench—named for the yarns local sportsman yield while sitting there—told him Buck was as tough as nails. But Glynn would be damned if the kid wasn't the hammer.

"Don't know what I was expecting," Buck continued, "but a guy in a trash bag wasn't it. I just stood there, you know, not sure what to do. With the weather we been havin', figured he'd done froze to death. But then he moved and it nearly put a load in my pants. Just his shoulder that was sticking out, just a little bit, see."

"See what?" James asked.

"Nothing. He didn't get up or anything. At that point, I didn't know if he knew I was there or not. So I yelled to him, 'Hey, you okay? Do you need help?' But the guy didn't respond, so I yelled again. 'I see you behind the tree. I can help you.' And still nothing." Buck peered over at the store. "I was only about the distance from us to the front door there, so I'd say about twenty feet. He must've heard me."

"But he didn't respond at all?" Glynn clarified.

"Nope. Not one bit."

"So what did you do then?" Garrett asked.

"I didn't have the foggiest idea what to do. Figured he was half a popsicle—that's just common sense, but I'd never seen anything like it. For all I knew this guy was straight from the looney bin. Or worse, packing heat. So I came here and called you guys."

"You did the right thing." James looked to the wardens. "What do you guys make of this?"

"To be honest," Glynn said, "I'm not sure if we're on a search and rescue or an apprehension. Something's just not adding up. If the guy was trying to survive, why didn't he stay in the cabin?"

"And why didn't he use the door after breaking in the first time?" Garrett added.

"I would have taken the booze," Buck said.

"Right. Seems like all cards are on the table." Glynn looked at Buck. The kid was close to six feet tall and rugged. He'd probably spent as many nights in the woods as they did—heck, he'd make a good warden. So if he was weirded out by the man, there was something unsettling about the whole situation. "Other than the trash bag, could you tell what he was wearing for clothing?"

"Nope. All I could see was a bulge in the garbage bag that I think was his right arm. Looked like he'd only cut a hole for his head."

"We have to assume he's hypothermic," Garrett said. "That might explain the erratic behavior."

"So what's the plan?" James wanted to know.

"Just a minute." Garrett went to his truck and came back with a Delorme, which he laid out on the hood of James's cruiser. He shined his Kel-Lite onto the map. "Buck, show me where the camp is."

Buck pointed to a cove on the southwest corner of the lake, just north of an outlet.

"Okay," Garrett said. "We're about fifteen miles from the northern end of the lake now. Is snowmobiling from there the best way to get to the cabin?"

"That's how I do it," Buck said. "Left my sled at the end of a logging road over there."

"Perfect. We're gonna need you to show us where you saw the man. Since he didn't react to you earlier, chances are he's still in the area, if not the cabin. James, you can ride with me. Before we go on the lake, we'll disconnect the headlights to all sleds but one. This way the man will likely think it's Buck coming back to the cabin, and he won't be worried about us."

From the boat launch, Glynn led the three-snowmobile caravan across the lake. The air temperature had dropped into the negative teens, and the fierce headwind was brutal. It was a four-mile ride across the lake, and while Glynn's department-issued down parka and wool pants were doing an admirable job of fighting off the cold, his fingers and toes were stinging from the early going. This didn't bode well for their mystery man. What was the chance he was still alive?

As Glynn's sled approached the shore, something moved along the tree line. Glynn gunned the snowmobile into the woods, where he spotted a man grab something from the ground and retreat into the thicket. Without bothering to hit the kill switch, Glynn ejected himself from the sled and gave pursuit. It was a dense area of cedar and spruce that was like running through a football line of scrimmage. Glynn held his forearms before his face and barreled through the trees. Snow spilled from the branches into his collar, sending an icy chill down his back.

Glynn stopped to get his bearings. The mystery man could be heard crashing through the forest to his left. The man had switched directions, and by the sound of it, Glynn wasn't any closer to him than when he'd jumped off his sled. Following the tracks wasn't going to work, the man was too fast. Instead, Glynn charged ahead in the direction of the crashing sounds, stopping every so often to listen and redirect. It was a cat and mouse pursuit that was enabling Glynn to cut the corners off each turn. Slowly but surely he was getting closer. At one point, Glynn must have stopped at the same time as the man because there weren't any sounds to follow. Glynn waited. And waited. Then, all of a sudden, there was commotion behind him and an approaching light. Glynn slid his hand over his pistol, just in case.

Buck emerged from between the branches of a spruce tree. "Holy hell! Don't shoot, I'm on your side." He cracked a sly grin. "This time, anyway."

At that moment, there was a loud snap of a branch, followed by more crashing. They were close.

"Go back!" Glynn told Buck. Without waiting to see if he obeyed, Glynn took off after the man, continuing his stop-and-go strategy. The closer Glynn got, the more he stopped. Then Glynn noticed snow falling from a tree. He lunged into the branches and nearly fell coming out the other side. Before him, a man was hung up in an opposing thicket.

"Don't move!" Glynn tried to yell, but the sounds coming out of his mouth were a poor resemblance. He gasped for air. "Warden service!"

Glynn directed his light upon a tall skeleton of a man, who looked to be in his late thirties, maybe early forties, with a scruffy beard that was a mix of white and fire-red whiskers. He was wearing a gray hard-hat liner for a hat, a lightweight shell in lieu of a winter jacket, blue jeans that were raggedy and stained, old work boots, and brown leather gloves. How he was surviving in this ensemble was anyone's guess. Perhaps the answer was in the half-full garbage bag slung over his shoulder?

"Don't move," Glynn said. He held the flashlight up with his left hand while his right slid over his pistol, ready to draw if necessary. Glynn took a cautious step toward the man, who reacted by slowly sliding his right hand down his side.

"Don't move!"

Glynn shined the light at the man's back pocket. A silver ice pick was sticking out. Glynn unholstered his pistol and aimed it at the man. The last thing he wanted to do was shoot, but that decision might be made for him.

"I said don't move! If you move, I will shoot."

The man froze in place.

Glynn took another step toward him, and once again the man tried for his ice pick.

"Don't move!"

Glynn aimed the pistol at the man's chest.

He froze.

Glynn inched another step forward.

The man's hand inched closer to his back pocket.

"Damn it, I said don't move!"

At this point, Trooper Townsend arrived at the scene. He, too, was short of breath.

"Thank goodness," James said, panting. "How's it going?"

"He responds to my commands," Glynn said. "But when I approach him, he tries for the ice pick in his back pocket. I think if you go around from behind, we can subdue him peacefully without anyone getting hurt." Glynn said this loud enough for the man to hear.

"Sounds good," James said. He started to circle the man.

"Don't move," Glynn repeated. He aimed his Kel-Lite at the man's face. This time, the man didn't try for the ice pick. He merely looked back at Glynn with an empty stare. James moved in and slid the ice pick out of his pocket without incident. He then cuffed the man.

"Who are you?" the man demanded.

"Maine Warden Service," Glynn said.

"Who are you?"

"I just told you."

"Who are you? Who are you? Who are you!"

"He's Sergeant Preston from her Majesty's Royal Mounties," James said. "Can't you tell by the puffy jacket?"

"I know who you are," the man said.

"Congratulations," Glynn said. "Now will you tell us who you are?"

"I know who you are."

"I'll take that as a no."

"Unidentified wild male," James said, deadpan. He took the garbage bag from the man and shined his light inside. "Sleeping bag . . . not a winter mummy . . . couple cans of beans . . . matches . . . another few trash bags . . . that's it."

"How long have you been out here?" Glynn asked. "Are you hurt?"

"I know who you are. You're from Telstar!"

"How about frostbite? Can you feel your hands and toes?"

"You're from Telstar. Go back to Telstar!"

"Well," James said, "we know you can run, so let's see how you walk. Follow Sergeant Preston out and I'll be right behind you, so no funny business. I have a gun, too."

James gave the man a nudge and he stepped forward. About halfway to the cabin, he started in again.

"I know you're from Telstar. Fly back to Telstar!"

"Keep walking, unidentified wild male," James said.

"Leave me alone. Fly back to Telstar. I am the woods. I care for the trees. Go back to Telstar. Me and the trees. This is my home. Go back to Telstar. Get out of my home. Leave me my trees. I know who you are. You're from Telstar. Fly back to Telstar!"

"Beam me up, Scotty," James said.

"Leave me my trees!"

Garrett and Buck were waiting for them at the cabin. By the time they got back, the man had calmed down. They agreed to handcuff him to the strap that went across the back of Garrett's snowmobile seat. After working up a sweat chasing the man, everyone was now cooling off quickly, so they didn't waste a minute milling around. James hopped on the sled with Glynn, who trailed Garrett's snowmobile to keep an eye on the wild man. Crossing the lake, Glynn noticed the tracks from Garrett's snowmobile turning black. While it had been below freezing for a full week, the temperatures before this spell had been mild, and it was clear they were traveling on thin ice. Glynn pulled up alongside Garrett's sled and motioned him to shore.

Close to shore, both wardens and James got off their sleds for a side conversation.

"Our sleds are breaking through," Glynn said to Garrett. "I can see water filling your tracks."

"There are no roads back from here," Garrett said. "We have to go down the lake, we'll just stick closer to shore."

Glynn nodded to the wild man. "What about him? We can't keep him cuffed to the sled."

"I know." Garrett looked the wild man over. "I don't like it, though."

"Me either." Glynn walked back to Garrett's sled and addressed the man. "We're traveling on thin ice. It's too dangerous to keep the handcuffs on, so we're going to take them off."

The wild man paid no attention to Glynn. They'd put a spare jacket and hat on him, which partially concealed his frail state. He sat there, rocking back and forth on the snowmobile seat. It was as if he was in another place altogether, his silence more disconcerting than the previous ranting.

"If you try to hurt Garrett," Glynn said, "I swear to the trees that I'll run you over with my sled. Do you understand?"

The man continued to rock.

Glynn looked to Garrett for help.

"He's in la la land," Garrett said. "I need confirmation."

"Listen," Glynn said more forcefully.

The man flinched.

He turned to Glynn. Bloodshot eyes and a sallow complexion made him look as though he hadn't slept in weeks.

"I'm going to take these off," Glynn said, gesturing to the cuffs. "You have to hold onto the snowmobile. I need you to stay safe. Don't try to get off the sled or hurt anyone. Do you understand?"

The man nodded.

"Good. Remember what I said."

The wild man was true to his nod, and the remaining ride across the lake and down several logging roads was uneventful. Back at the vehicles, they handcuffed the man and loaded him into Garrett's truck. Glynn rode with them to the Machias Jail. Both wardens had previously worked rescues on the Appalachian Trail's

100-Mile Wilderness, and so they were familiar with the ripe
stench of someone who'd been in the woods for days. They agreed
that a thru-hiker's odor was nothing compared to the foulness from
the wild man that filled the cabin of Garrett's truck, worsened by
the pumping heat. The inability to breathe put a damper on any
conversation. The wild man, to Glynn's disappointment, also held
quiet. There was one question Glynn wanted him to answer: *How
had he survived?*

~

The next morning, Glynn phoned the Inland Fisheries and Wildlife Department's safety officer. Glynn explained that the man
they'd found wasn't appropriately dressed for winter, and the sleeping bag he had was cheap and flimsy. The safety officer told him,
hypothetically, the man shouldn't have survived a single night in
the weather they were having. There must have been something
else keeping him alive.

Glynn and Garrett went back to the cabin to look for evidence
they might have missed at night. They found where the man had
bedded. There was a small fire pit, no more than a foot wide, with
several empty cans of food. The burn marks on the bottom of the
cans showed he was using the fire to cook food and probably not
much else. Given the small size, it wouldn't have provided enough
heat to keep him warm. Not in this weather, anyway. Where he
had bedded down, there was no sign of a snow cave, nor were there
any clipped spruce branches used for added insulation. His survival skills appeared non-existent, and yet, all the footprints, cans
of food, and yellow snow suggested he'd been there for a couple of
days.

"Could you have made it through a night like this?" Glynn
asked.

"Not a chance," Garrett said. "You'd have to be crazy to try it."

"That might be the best explanation we've got."

They weren't far from the truth. James informed them that the background check revealed the man had spent considerable time in a Virginia prison. They didn't get the full story, but he'd been involved in a homicide while behind bars, and apparently had suffered from PTSD ever since. Somehow he'd gotten released, after which he disappeared from his parole officer's purview. Luck also appeared to be on the wild man's side this time around. Due to a mix-up in court, he was once again released and free to be with the trees.

Glynn met Garrett for coffee a few months later.

"Did you hear the latest on our wild man from Fourth Machias Lake?" Garrett asked.

"He's back?"

"Yep. Got a call from James the other day, telling me that an off-duty statie was fishing an Atlantic salmon hole on the Machias River. After fishing, he decided to boat over to his friend's remote camp, and—"

"I'm sensing a pattern."

"Yep. I guess I don't need to tell you, but as he approached the cabin, he noticed our wild man inside. By the sounds of it, a pretty good wrestling match ensued, and the trooper eventually hog-tied him, got him down the river in his canoe, and brought him to the Machias Jail."

"So I guess that does it."

"I guess so."

"I'd still like to know how he survived."

"Me too, but he's not talking, and neither are the trees."

CHAPTER SIX

Stuck in the Mud

THE HORIZON'S ORANGE AND PINK GLOW FADED AWAY THROUGH the treetops as dusk staked its nightly claim. It was time to go to work. Warden Dennis McIntosh stepped out of his department truck to eye the remote Norridgewock field. It was the end of a rainy week in October of 1978, and the ground was sure to be soft. From what he could see in the dwindling light, it looked like another vehicle had recently driven into the field.

Several calls of night hunting in the area had already been reported this fall, and he'd made arrests here in previous years. To him, this field was akin to a fisherman's secret spot. After a week of foul weather, the deer would be out, and so, Dennis was betting, would the spotlights.

Armed with a concrete justification, he began backing his rear-wheel-drive GMC along the edge of the field. Of course, it's always easier for the reward to outweigh the risk before one gets stuck. In this case, the rationale dissolved the moment the truck's back wheels began to spin and the engine revved with each press of the gas pedal, all of which wasn't to be outdone by the taunting sound of mud slapping the flaps.

At least Dennis was alone. The last thing he wanted was an "I told you so" from the passenger seat. It didn't matter who you were, his warden brethren could be ruthless and relentless in these matters. There was no telling what hijinks would be coming his way should they find out. It would be best if he kept this to himself. So while he was confident he'd be able to get the truck unstuck without help, an uneasy *what if* lingered in the back of his mind.

Dennis retrieved his Handyman jack from the truck bed and positioned it under the rear trailer hitch. He pumped the handle until the back tires were a good foot off the ground, then he went around to the side of the truck and pushed it over and off the jack. The truck landed with the tires about six inches from the previous trenches. He repeated the process, hoping to get the tires far enough away to avoid getting stuck again. Satisfied with a foot of separation, he pulled his camouflage parachute over the truck. As he was doing this, a vehicle could be heard coming down the dirt road. Dennis quickly finished concealing the truck and lay in the wet grass with his binoculars trained on the road.

The approaching vehicle sounded like a beater of an old truck, its muffler rattling and roaring over every pothole in the road. Once it came into view, Dennis realized it was the mother ship of all cars, a large Oldsmobile sedan model from the sixties. The driver's window was open and facing the field, and someone in the front passenger seat was reaching over the top of the car to aim a flashlight. The beam was unsteady at best, bouncing every which way around the field. Unfortunately for the folks in the car, there was no sliding scale to reduce the violation for sloppy spotlighting.

Dennis burst into action as soon as the car passed, ripping the parachute off his truck and hopping into the front seat. He started the ignition and kept all lights—headlights, interior, and blues—off. In the excitement of the moment, he completely forgot about having been stuck and stomped on the gas. The back wheels started spinning and the truck began to fishtail. His only chance of catching the culprits was to gun it, so he cut the wheel into the slide and floored the gas pedal, watching as the RPM gauge shot into the red. The back tires continued to chuck topsoil until the truck was fully bogged down and stuck in the mud, again.

So much for that.

Dennis retrieved the Handyman jack. The ground squished and sucked at his boots with each step, and he slipped to his knees more than once. By the time he got the truck moved over and restarted, he was ready to be done with the evening. Slowly pressing on the gas pedal, the truck pulled out of the field without digging into the mud. There was no point going after the poachers now, so Dennis went home.

At least he didn't have to call for help.

— ~

Dennis returned to the same field the following evening. This time around, he parked on higher ground closer to the tree line. Shortly after he covered his truck with the parachute, he heard a rowdy car rattling down the road.

Sure enough, the same Oldsmobile came into view. Once again, the field was sprayed by an unsteady beam of light emitting from the top of the car. Dennis readied his truck for pursuit. Keeping all lights off, he slowly pulled out of the field without issue and turned onto the dirt road a short distance behind the car.

Dennis watched the car's rear lights to avoid potholes and prepare for upcoming turns in the road. The strategy behind going dark was to avoid a high-speed chase by surprising the other vehicle, but it certainly wasn't without danger. Anytime Dennis cut the lights, he couldn't help but think of a story his warden mentor, Harold Emery, once passed along. Harold had been on a similar dark pursuit when the poachers he was tailing, unbeknownst to him, had also killed their car's lights. At the time, they didn't know a vehicle was coming from behind, and they inexplicably stopped in the middle of the road. Even after Harold's truck crashed into the back of the car, it took the driver a bit to realize what happened. When Harold came around the front see if everyone was okay, the driver exclaimed, "Thank goodness you're here—the trunk of my car just exploded!"

While tales such as these helped inspire Dennis to become a warden, he had no desire to recreate the scene. Getting closer to the car, he could see the road well enough in the glow of the taillights to feel safe from reenactment; however, it wasn't out of the question that the car would break down before him. Plumes of exhaust billowed from the tailpipe, which hung only an inch or two above the ground.

When Dennis flicked on the truck's lights and activated the flashing blues, the car made a sudden swerve in the road before slowing to a stop. He parked behind the vehicle, and from what he could see in his truck's headlights, there were two people in the front seats. The driver was making a jerking motion. Dennis had seen this many times before—the driver was unloading a gun. He approached the vehicle and shined his flashlight in the car. Behind the wheel sat a man in his mid-thirties. A .30-30 Winchester was on the floor beneath his legs, and there were several brass cartridges scattered around his feet. The rifle was pointing up toward the passenger seat, where a woman nervously clutched a flashlight between her knees. She'd forgotten to turn it off, and for good reason. It was likely the gun had been pointed in her direction when the man ejected the bullets, making for an extremely dangerous situation.

A voice in the back seat caught Dennis by surprise. Two young boys were sitting in back, both too short to have been seen from behind the vehicle. The oldest couldn't have been more than six years old. Now Dennis was walking the fine line between lecturing the parents for their negligence, and keeping a calm presence to avoid upsetting the kids. He took a deep breath.

"What are you folks up to tonight?" Dennis asked, fully expecting a cockamamie explanation.

The driver sat there with his hands on the wheel and his mouth half-cocked, as if his jaw had broken the sound barrier and he was waiting for the words to catch up.

The oldest of the two boys filled the void. "We're looking for deer!"

"Is that so?" Dennis said with a laugh. There's something to be said about cooperation. Even if it comes from unexpected places.

CHAPTER SEVEN

Aroostook County Search Warrant

NAT BERRY FOUND HIS OFFICE IN DISARRAY. HE'D ONLY BEEN OUT a few minutes, and in this time, the nameplate on his desk had been tipped over, the previously neatly stacked paperwork scattered about, and, by the looks of it, someone had sat in his chair and propped their muddy boots on the desk, kicking off plenty of dirt.

Nat sighed. No doubt, the culprit had dumped a pail of water outside to create the muck that was now soaking into the paperwork. And was that a blade of grass circling around in his coffee? Nat liked things neat and proper. Order and structure helped him focus on the tasks at hand. It was something he'd learned in the military, and he failed to see how this was a crime, but for some reason, the rest of the Warden Service deemed disrupting his tidiness part of their civic duty. It wasn't just the men and women who reported to him, either. Nat's supervisor, Russ Dyer, was always dismayed by Nat's clean and polished appearance. On one occasion, Russ pulled his vehicle alongside Nat's and slammed open his truck door, leaving a dent and a sizeable white scrape on Nat's door. "There," Russ proclaimed. "Now it looks like a warden truck."

A rap on the doorframe caught Nat's attention.

"Hey, Sarg," Ben Fortin, district warden for the Bridgeton area, said.

"Did you—" Nat started to say before catching himself. He knew Ben wasn't a prankster.

"Looks like wardens being wardens in here," Ben said.

"Yeah." Then it hit him. The perpetrator was a known delinquent in these matters. "Dyer."

"That'd be my guess."

"I'll fix him," Nat said. "What brings you around?"

"I was talking to my informant this morning, and he told me about this guy from Waterford, Mack Barnum, an independent logger who shot a moose from his truck the other day. It's one of those things where my guy heard it from a friend of a friend, so I don't think we have enough to get a warrant."

"Not without a signed statement from someone with firsthand knowledge."

"Which we can't get without exposing my informant as a snitch. I really don't want to do that; he's been too helpful. But I also don't want to drop it. My guy swears it's true and he hasn't misled us yet."

"Do you know where the moose is?"

"Not really. I assume Mack has it at his house, but he might not."

Nat glanced at his watch. "It's almost five now. Why don't we go to Mack's place tonight and have a look around? If the situation is right, we can call in an Aroostook County search warrant."

Ben raised his eyebrows. "You know, for such a neat freak, you can sure play warden dirty."

"It's all by the book." Nat grabbed the phone. "Let's see if Molly is on tonight." He called dispatch. Molly had just begun her shift. After exchanging pleasantries, Nat said to her, "We might need your help tonight on an Aroostook County search warrant."

"Oh really," she said. "I'm a little out of practice. Not sure I still know what to say."

"It's like riding a bicycle."

"What's the guy's name?"

"Mack Barnum from Waterford. He shot a moose."

"Hello, Mack." Molly lowered her voice to a hushed tone as if she was trying to avoid being overheard. "This is Tina from the Naples Diner. You don't know me, but there were some wardens in here tonight, and I heard them talking. They're on their way to your place now and they've got a warrant for the moose you shot. Good luck. Those bastards are lousy tippers." Molly went silent for a second. "And that's when I hang up."

"You've still got it, but do you have to be so disparaging?"

"Nat, I've got to sell it."

"Yeah, well, just for the record, we are lousy tippers."

Molly laughed. "Why am I not surprised? Give me a second and I'll bring up Mack's info." Nat could hear her pounding away on the keyboard. "Okay, here it is." She relayed Mack's address and phone number.

After hanging up with Molly, Nat turned to Ben. "Give Brad a call and see if he's available tonight. Let's break for dinner and we'll meet up at the Naples warden camp at eight. We can all head over from there."

Joined by Deputy Warden Brad St. Peter, it was a little after nine when they drove past the suspect's house and parked at a turnoff down the road.

"Where's the parachute?" Ben wanted to know. "We can't get away without it tonight. You've got this truck so polished up, it will reflect light from an owl's eyes. It's no wonder Dyer dented the door—I have half a mind to mud it up right now."

"Don't you dare," Nat said. "Unless you want to be on nuisance wildlife duty for a month."

It was a mild and overcast night, making a silent approach through the woods challenging without the use of flashlights. Their prowess for being wardens was judged among themselves by their nighttime stealth abilities. Needless to say, they took turns chiding each other for snapping sticks.

Mack had a long dirt driveway that came in beside a small ranch house. From the tree line, the wardens were facing the side of the house, where there was a sliding glass door with half-drawn curtains. A light was on inside and it appeared as though they were looking in on the kitchen table. The funny thing with the glass door was that it was about three to four feet off the ground with no porch or steps, so it apparently wasn't used as a regular entrance. But it would have made for a perfect spot to back up a truck and unload the moose.

Ben must have been thinking the same thing. "I'll check the truck for evidence." As soon as he said this, two geese ambled around the corner of the house and began honking at them. The three men scurried for cover. Ben ran for Mack's Ford F-150, Nat ducked behind a rusted-out Jeep on blocks, and Brad chose an adjacent pine.

"Great," Brad whispered. "Guard geese."

This was a first. Clearly agitated, the geese continued to honk and strut around in an erratic pattern as if they didn't quite know what to do about the wardens' presence. From this respect, it was a stalemate. Fortunately, the geese didn't attack any of the wardens or do anything to disclose their hiding spots—other than making a ruckus, that is.

A dark figure briefly passed the sliding glass door, but nobody looked out. Whoever was home either couldn't hear the geese, which was hard to fathom, or more likely didn't care. The incessant honking may have been a common occurrence.

Nat radioed dispatch. "Tell my A-unit I want to be home," he said, code for Molly to place the call. Soon afterward, a man holding a phone receiver to his ear came to the glass door and pulled back the curtain. A spotlight flashed on and Nat instinctively lowered his head. The light stayed on for roughly thirty seconds of actual time, which translated to five minutes of heart-pounding anticipation. Then it went out. A moment later, the man who'd been on the phone, presumably Mack, came out a back door with a .30-06 rifle in his hands. He was wearing jeans and a gray pullover, but with the lights out, Nat couldn't get a good look at his face. Average in height, Mack's broad shoulders fit the lumberjack profile.

Mack's reputation in the dooryard preceded him; the geese honked and scampered at his sudden appearance. He walked through the darkness in the direction of Nat and Brad.

Keeping low, Nat circled around the Jeep as Mack passed. From his crouched position, Nat had a limited view under the Jeep, and he watched as Mack's unlaced steel-toe boots approached the giant tires of a skidder. Nat slowly stood up for a better view. The Jeep had a soft top, and through the cloudy, plastic back window, he could faintly see Mack at the skidder. Mack was standing with his back to Nat, and his shoulders blocked the view, so Nat couldn't see what he was doing. Mack glanced over his shoulder, then headed back to the house. He was no longer carrying the rifle.

"I thought he was coming for us," Nat whispered to Brad after hearing the back door close.

"Me too," Brad replied. "I was about to draw."

"Did you see what he did with the rifle?"

"I did." Ben crept over to them from his hiding spot. "He removed one of the skidder's side plates and tucked the rifle inside."

"He's expecting us to arrive soon," Nat said, "so let's get the truck."

"I'll grab the rifle," Ben said.

"Careful," Nat told him. "Don't make any noise 'til we get back."

Once they got the truck, Nat drove it up the long driveway so their arrival could be seen from the sliding-glass door. He and Brad got out, half expecting to be attacked by geese, but the birds were nowhere to be seen. They knocked on the back door, and after a few seconds of waiting, the light came on. The man they'd seen hide the rifle answered, and as far as they could tell, nobody else was home. He looked to be in his mid-thirties with blue eyes, dirty-blond hair, and a scraggly beard. Having the advantage of being a step higher, he towered over them.

"Are you Mack Barnum?" Nat asked.

The man nodded. "Yep."

"We'd like to talk to you about the moose."

"What moose?"

"The one you shot Wednesday out of your truck."

"The only gun I keep in the truck is my .44 Magnum. I've got a permit for it. Here, I'll show you." Mack led them to his truck, where he opened the passenger door and produced both the revolver and the concealed weapons permit. "Did you collect any casings from the scene?"

"We did," Brad said, bluffing.

"Bet they don't match this gun."

"Actually," Ben said from behind them, holding up the .30-06. "We'd like to talk to you about shooting the moose with *this* gun."

Mack's face dropped. "What can I say?" he said with a shrug. "You got me."

Ben nudged Nat. "Your kind of night," he said. "He came clean."

Chapter Eight

What Happened to Ludger Belanger?

Lieutenant Warden John Marsh tipped back his coffee mug, an act of bleary-eyed wishful thinking, considering he'd emptied it two hours before. He and District Warden Richard "Dick" Hennessy had been working all night knocking on doors and searching the surrounding woods for a missing hunter, twenty-five-year-old Ludger Belanger of Washington. The two wardens were now warming themselves in John's department-issued cruiser, jotting down their activity report notes, and pondering their next move. It was Wednesday, November 26, 1975.

"Something's not right," John said, slapping the topographical map spread across the dashboard. Before transferring to the field in 1973, John had overseen the department's hunter safety program since 1966, where he investigated hunting accidents and developed statewide policies. "This just doesn't make any sense. How does a young man, by all accounts fit and healthy, practically hunting in his own backyard, go lost? Seems unlikely he'd get hurt in terrain like this—it's all flat."

"I agree," Dick said. He was peering out the window, his dark hair and olive complexion a stark contrast to the snow-covered landscape. Despite having worked all night, Dick's trademark flat-top didn't have a hair out of place. Like John, he was thirty-three years old. He'd worked the field since joining the Warden Service in 1964, and John trusted his detective instincts. "If you ask me, our best bet is to park in his driveway and wait for him to come home. He's bound to sober up sooner or later."

Dick was joking, but not really. Given the situation, it seemed the most plausible scenario, which in part explained why only two wardens were searching for a missing person who may have spent a cold November night in the woods. The foot of snow that had blanketed the region in the past twenty-four hours didn't help, either. Thanksgiving was still a day away, but the true day of thanks for Maine hunters in an era when many relied on hunting to put meat on the table was the first snowfall of the season, which also made it one of the craziest days for wardens. The department's resources were stretched thin, and reports of a truckload of deer being smuggled out of state was the hot assignment. John and Dick were there mostly for due diligence, and until they could prove Ludger Belanger was safe and sound, they still had diligence to do.

Normally clean-shaven, John scratched his stubbly face and ran his hand over his buzz cut. "Everything we know about this job wants me to agree with you, but Ludger's wife was ready to swear on the Bible that the drunk shoe didn't fit."

John and Dick had visited the Belanger house on Tuesday night. As they stood inside the doorway speaking to Ludger's wife, Linda, the two oldest of the couple's three daughters clung to their mother's legs. John was six feet tall and 220 pounds, and with Dick at his side, the two wardens in their uniforms must have been an intimidating presence. Still, it didn't take long before curiosity drew the girls to them, where they playfully picked snowballs from John and Dick's boots.

At twenty years of age, Linda looked very much a kid herself. Cradling her four-month-old in her arms, she admirably kept herself together while explaining to the girls that the wardens were going to bring their daddy home.

The conviction in her voice didn't seem as strong as she recalled how she, Ludger, his oldest brother, and his father, had all gone hunting at daybreak. Despite their strength in numbers, luck wasn't on their side. The fast-falling snow concealed any deer activity from overnight, and they weren't fortunate enough to happen upon any fresh tracks. Ludger was between jobs, so when it came time for his father and brother to reluctantly report to work, he had Linda drop him off at a field about a mile from their house. Linda returned home for the morning routine with the girls and to get ready for her midday waitressing shift. She didn't drive in snow, so the plan was for Ludger to hunt his way home by noon so he could take her to work.

When Ludger didn't show, Linda was furious. There was no doubt in her mind he'd gotten onto a fresh track he couldn't quit. By the time darkness fell, her frustration had turned to concern, and when a family search party came up empty, she called the authorities. This wasn't like him, she said several times, her voice cracking a bit more with each reiteration.

John had met enough potential widows to know her mind was racing with worst-case scenarios every time her eyes flashed upon the girls.

"Linda was very convincing," he said.

"She was," Dick agreed. "The neighbors all said the same: straight as an arrow, never misses church. Then again, sometimes those are the guys you have to watch. But let's suppose he didn't get into the hooch. Maybe Linda was right when she said he probably got onto a fresh track? Perhaps he even shot and wounded the deer? If you were him, how far would you follow it?"

"All night. A good size buck could feed their family for the winter."

"So maybe he just got too far away to get back before nightfall? I don't care how well you know these woods, once it's dark, all bets are off. Especially in a storm with the wind blowing as it has been. And if he didn't have a light. . . ."

"It's as good a theory as any. It might explain why he didn't respond to the gunshots from his family's search party." John sighed. "At this point, we can't rule anything out. God help him if he did go out and tie one on. We might have to put the poor boy into protective custody. Not that the alternative is rosy. We have to assume he wasn't equipped for a night in the woods and by now is likely hypothermic."

"So what now? Are we going to call in the troops?"

John had a decision to make. He could call for a search party, bringing in any available law enforcement, firefighters, volunteers—anybody and everybody—to canvass the area. They'd conduct a line search, where a group of people comb the woods in a straight line, each person within sight of the next. While more eyeballs would increase the odds of finding Ludger, the approach wasn't without risk. A large group untrained in wilderness search and rescue was just as likely to trample evidence than to find it. Whether anyone believed Ludger was in the woods or not was irrelevant. John had to assume he was, and that the situation was life threatening.

"We don't have time to organize a search. If Ludger's out there, and he's alive, he won't be for long. Besides, at this point, we don't even know where to send people to look." John grabbed the two-way radio. "I'll see if we can get a couple more wardens out here. For now, our best bet is for you and me to find his tracks. Pronto."

The decision was ripe for second guessing, but it felt right. For his part, Dick didn't argue with the plan. They were parked where Linda said she'd left Ludger, in an area with fields on both sides of the road. The snow had begun falling in the wee hours of the morning, with a good six to eight inches already accumulated, when Ludger ventured into the field around 8 a.m. At about the same time, a sudden blast of cold arctic air changed the snowfall from heavy and wet to a light fluff. John and Dick knew Ludger's tracks were likely preserved in a layer of frozen slush; if only they could find them under the subsequent four inches of powder. The Belanger family had also conducted their search on snowmobiles, so there was a good chance they'd driven over his tracks. John and Dick began by pacing the roadside, looking for any clues. It wasn't out of the question that the town plow truck could have turned up a shell casing or something else Ludger might have dropped. This was truly a needle-in-a-haystack type of search.

Shortly after they began checking the roadside, a man emerged from a nearby house. They'd knocked on the door the night before, but no one had answered. The man, who looked to be in his late thirties, approached the wardens. His old bomber hat, tattered flannel shirt, and stained wool pants all suggested deep woodsman's roots.

"Whatcha looking for?" the man wanted to know.

John took the lead explaining the situation. After a night of going door to door, his spiel was well rehearsed.

The man identified himself as Clayton Crosby. "But you can just call me Clay—everybody does. I can tell you exactly where Ludger went. I seen him out my kitchen window go into the woods in the back corner of that field right there."

"Are you sure it was Ludger Belanger?"

"Not a hundred percent. I didn't go out and shake his hand or anything, but it was him. I recognized his red and black checkered jacket. He hunts in there quite a bit. I see him coming and going. There are a few other guys that go in there, but it's mostly him. I do a good bit of hunting and trapping in there myself, and if you go in a ways, there's a little ridge that follows a stream. It's a good place to hunt. Buncha beech trees. Deer travel through there to the fields. If I were him, that's where I woulda been headed." Clay paused. "Tell you what, I was about to go hunting now myself, but I'd be happy to help look for him. He's a good kid."

John accepted Clay's offer.

One of the snowmobile tracks led the three men across the field to where Clay said Ludger had gone into the woods. It was a crisp morning and the sled-packed snow crunched beneath their boots. The three men spread out as they entered the tree line at the crest of a rolling hill. John was in the middle following the snowmobile track, while the other two stayed within sight of him. The deer had been active overnight, leaving a maze of crisscrossing prints. John couldn't help but think there'd been no daytime tracks when Ludger had passed through.

Eventually, the snowmobile track turned and headed in the direction of the Belanger residence. Clay urged them to keep to their present course, insisting they were almost to the ridge. They took his advice and when they got to the ridge, there was no immediate sign of Ludger, but it felt like they were getting close. The ridge was the one spot where a hunter could get the high-ground advantage, and the surrounding hardwoods offered decent firing lanes. This had to be where he was going.

Dick worked his way along the ridge. He stopped walking and called over to John. By the time John joined him, he'd dusted out three frozen boot prints. The tracks were close together, no doubt the slow, deliberate gait of a hunter.

"This has to be our guy," John said.

They followed the tracks along the ridge, which was slightly windswept from the storm. The prints were completely uncovered in some places and buried under several inches of powder in others. Every so often, Ludger appeared to come to a standstill, and in one of these spots, a flash of gold caught John's eye.

"What have we here?" John reached into the snow and fished out two spent .30-30 cartridges. The three men instinctively followed Ludger's tracks with their eyes. Moving ahead, they found where the deer was shot, and John instructed Clay to stand back as the wardens inspected the evidence. It was a crusted-over spot, and there were a few blood splatters that had soaked through the snow, leaving a trail Ludger could have followed. Upon cresting the ridge, they found a dark pool of frozen blood and guts where Ludger had dressed the deer. There was also another shell casing at this location, likely the finishing shot.

"It was a buck," Dick said, nudging the frozen scrotum with the toe of his boot.

"A big one at that," Clay added. Stationed a few feet off to the side, he was digging out the deer's tracks with his fingers. "Quite the trophy by the looks of this."

"Is that a second person?" Dick asked. He was pointing out two sets of footprints, one coming and one going, on each side of the drag trail. They could also see imprints where the deer had been dragged over the tracks of the person pulling it. Dick knelt down for a closer inspection. "I don't know, both sets might be Ludger's. I'll take a look." He followed the drag trail until he was well out of sight before returning to the group. "They're definitely all Ludger's tracks. What he did was walk his gun ahead, rest it against a tree, and then return for the deer. Looks like he kept repeating this pattern."

"Why would he drag the deer south?" John asked. "His house is north of here."

"The old Creamer Lot Road is about a quarter of a mile that way," Clay said. "It's just a woods road now, but it's drivable, so if he got the deer out to it, he could have gone for help."

"Makes sense," John said. "The obvious question now is why didn't anyone hear from him? Even if he was going to drag it out entirely by himself, a good-sized deer like that deserves some bragging rights." John thought on it for a moment. "Where does the road come out on the other end?"

"It doesn't. Dead ends at an old gravel pit."

"Alright then, it sounds like we need to secure the entry of that road. Dick, you and Clay follow the drag trail out to the road. See what you can find. Clay, if you see anything, don't touch it without Dick's say-so."

"Understood."

"Okay. I'll walk back out to block the road and see if anyone else has arrived."

Warden Earl Kelly was waiting at the main road. John brought him up to speed on the situation and they drove their cruisers to the end of the woods road. There were no footprints or drag marks to be seen, but a vehicle had gone in and come out at some point during the storm the previous day. They blocked the road's entry with their cruisers, John grabbed his camera, and together they walked in to meet Dick and Clay. They found them about a quarter mile in, inspecting a spot where the vehicle had stopped.

"What have you got?" John asked.

"The vehicle stopped here," Dick said. "Apparently to pick up Ludger's gun."

"Was Ludger in the vehicle?"

"I believe so. There's another spot where they stopped about a hundred yards up the road and he got in. I can tell by the way the tracks cross over each other that the vehicle drove in before Ludger reached the road and met him on the way out. There were at least two people in the vehicle: the driver and another male in the front passenger seat, who I think has a cane. Both of them got out to take a leak back there where they met Ludger. The driver helped Ludger load the deer into the rear of the vehicle and it appears as though Ludger got in the back seat."

Dick pointed to John's camera. "Good. There's a couple things here you're going to want to get a picture of. Look over here where the driver got out of the car." He gestured to a cigarette butt in the snow.

"The cigarette?" John asked, unsure it was what Dick intended.

"Yeah. The driver also discarded one back where they picked Ludger up. It's only a thirty-second drive from there to here. Both cigarettes were smoked down to the filter."

"They took their time."

"Right. You're also gonna want to follow the driver's footprints."

John could see that the driver had walked around the front of the vehicle to a tree on the other side of the road. There was an imprint in the snow at the base of the tree where Ludger had left his gun, along with only one set of Ludger's footprints coming and going. The driver appeared to be wearing snowmobile boots, and his tracks were much larger than Ludger's, which made it easy to distinguish one from the other.

"Why did the driver retrieve Ludger's gun? If he was driving, it would have been easier for Ludger to get out."

"That's what I was wondering."

"Was there any other evidence at the first stop?" Earl asked.

"Yes. The driver also discarded a Budweiser can."

"And you said both guys got out of the vehicle to take a leak?"

"Yes."

"So they were probably half-cocked to begin with?"

"At least. That'd be my bet."

"John," Earl said, "I thought you told me Ludger doesn't drink."

"He doesn't."

"Well, maybe he didn't know he was drinking?" Earl said. "They could have offered him a thermos spiked with coffee brandy. That could have gotten him feeling pretty good before he realized what was happening."

"Or maybe he accepted a drink willingly?" Dick suggested. "Perhaps he thought a congratulatory beer wouldn't be a big deal, but if these were guys he knew, one beer might have loosened him up enough to be talked into a night of hell-raising."

"All of this is very plausible," John said, "but it doesn't explain why the driver got the gun. Even a drunk man wants to carry his own. It's what keeps us in business."

"It's odd," Earl agreed.

The group made their way to the pickup spot, where they could see Ludger had dragged the deer down the center of the road and pulled it off to the side when the car approached. As Dick described, two people—both likely men by the size of their boot prints—got out and relieved themselves. The passenger had shuffled through the snow, dragging his left foot sideways, and there were circular prints from what was probably a cane. The driver paced around a bit before joining Ludger at the deer, where it appeared the two men dragged it to the back of the vehicle and loaded it in. There was no sign of struggle. Ludger likely got into the vehicle of his own accord, as his tracks disappeared where one would imagine the driver-side backdoor being.

John was kneeling down to take a photo of the Budweiser can when Clay called to him.

"What is it?" John asked.

"I don't know," Clay said. "I was trying to move off the road to stay out of the way and I heard something crunch beneath my foot. Looks like a yellow piece of paper buried in the snow."

John took a photo of the paper before pulling it out. "You guys aren't going to believe this," he said. "It's a receipt from Sully's garage in Union, and it's dated for yesterday. The vehicle is a 1965 Buick Special owned by a man named Wayne Franklin. He's from Camden—we have both his address and phone number here."

"Great," Dick said. "Let's pay ol' Franklin a visit."

"Not yet," John said. "Something's not adding up. I can't get past the fact the driver retrieved the gun. Not to mention it has almost been twenty-four hours since Ludger was picked up—why hasn't he called his wife? I think we need to see if Linda knows Franklin before we stir that hornets' nest. I'm also going to get Sergeant Crabtree in here to work with the State Police on taking snow measurements and plaster casts of the boot prints and tire tracks before it all melts. Earl, I'd like you to wait at the end of the road for them to get here and stay there throughout. Make sure no one else comes in."

"You got it," Earl said.

On the way out, John thanked Clay for his help and instructed him to not talk about what they'd found with anyone, including Ludger's family. He agreed, saying he was going to go hunting behind his house to avoid the temptation.

"Be safe," John said.

Dick knocking on the Belanger's front door gave John a tinge of déjà-vu. The sound of his rapping set forth a familiar ovation inside the house from the girls' pattering feet and shrieking voices. As he waited, John stared at the same white paint flakes peeling away from the door frame that he had the night before. This time, it was the oldest girl who answered, sporting the now familiar bright smile and wavy brown hair John recognized from the picture he'd been provided of Ludger. It was a photo of him and Linda locked together, proudly displaying partridges they'd bagged earlier that fall.

"Mommy," she yelled over her shoulder, "the wabbon man's here." Then she turned her attention to John. "Where's daddy?"

Linda appeared before John could respond. Once again rocking her infant in her arms, she quickly ushered her eldest girl inside.

"We're sorry to stop by unannounced," John said.

"It's quite alright."

They all stood there for a moment, each hoping the other side had good news.

"Have you heard from your husband?" John asked.

Linda shook her head no.

"We came by in hopes that you could tell us who Wayne Franklin is?"

The blank stare on Linda's face told the wardens all they needed to know.

Sully's garage was the next stop. John and Dick agreed they needed to fill in as much backstory as they could before confronting Franklin. They both already knew Sully as an easy-going fellow who would be good for a few laughs and whatever information he had. There was no way they could have predicted his demeanor on this day.

"That no good son of a bitch!" Sully yelled at the mention of Franklin. A short, bald man with a bulky build and a panther tattoo on his left arm, he'd been working under the hood of a Bronco. "I hope to hell I never see that rotten piece of shit again."

"What happened?" John asked.

"He came in here yesterday at nine in the morning, already half in the bag, demanding we work on his junk car right then and there."

"The Buick?"

"Yes." Sully threw his hands in the air as he spoke. "The radiator was leaking and the car was full of steam. We couldn't fix it. We told him we couldn't fix it, but he wouldn't take no for an answer, so we tried to do what we could before sending him on his way. Well . . . he was back here at two even drunker than before, and you'll never guess what he did.

"The garage door was open and that son of a bitch backed his car right up onto the platform. Again yelling and swearing that we had to fix it, calling us no-good crooks, saying we cheated him. I've been doing this for thirty years and I've never seen anything like it. His car was all steamed up—I'm tellin' you, it was wall to wall, you could barely see inside the damn thing. I don't know how he was even able to drive it here. The real kicker was they never got out. They stayed in the car the whole time we worked on it. He even paid us out the window as if we're the drive-thru at fucking McDonald's."

"How many people were in the car?"

Sully closed the Bronco's lid and grabbed a rag for his hands. "Two. Franklin and some squirrelly looking guy in the passenger seat. He didn't say much to us. Just sat there drinking his beer and cracking jokes with Franklin."

"What does Franklin look like?"

"Oh, he's got dark hair, cut fairly short. Probably in his late twenties. I didn't look closely but I'd guess brown eyes. What I remember most is he had thick eyebrows. Real thick. He also hadn't shaved in two or three days. I'm tellin' you, the guy looks like a real a-hole."

"Noted," John said. "Do you have any idea how tall he is?"

Sully looked at John. "He's about your height, maybe an inch or two taller."

"What was he wearing?"

"All I saw was a forest green wool coat."

"What about the squirrelly guy?" Dick asked.

"He had a full, reddish-brown beard with long, greasy hair that came down over his shoulders. I'd guess he's also in his late twenties. Much shorter than the driver. He also had a cane with him. I think he was handicapped in some way. He was wearing a green Army jacket with an orange winter hat."

"An Army jacket?" Dick questioned. "Did you see the name on it?"

"No, sorry."

"Did you look in the back seat," John asked.

"I suppose I did, but I didn't make a point of it. The radiator is in the front."

"Is it possible someone could have been lying down sleeping and you didn't see him?"

"Nobody in their right mind would have been sleeping in that car. The steam went away soon after it was shut off and the guys inside weren't exactly being discreet. They were loud and drunk the whole time. If someone else were in there, we would have noticed."

"What about the deer in the trunk?"

"We didn't open the trunk. They said they'd been hunting, but I got the impression they hadn't had any luck. They were laughing and complaining that there aren't any deer in the whole county, saying they'd have better luck shooting something in our garage."

Sully gently kicked at the Bronco's front tire and continued in a quieter voice, "To be honest with you, they were making me nervous. There was a single-barrel shotgun lodged between them in the front seat and a five-pack of ammo on the dashboard. I half expected them to take target practice in here, so I distracted them with a *Parts Pups* mag. If you ask me, whatever hunting they did, I'd bet it was from the front seat of that car. Given how drunk they were when they first came in, they'd probably been out all night working the fields."

"I don't doubt it. Did you notice the make and model of the gun?"

"Not the make, but I assume the gun was a 12-gauge because the ammo was a box of Federal, 12-gauge, double-aught."

"Were any of the shells spent?"

"I don't know. The box was closed."

"Was there a .30-30 anywhere in the car? The back seat, perhaps?"

Sully shrugged. "I don't know. I'm sorry, guys; I was just trying to get them the hell out of here as fast as I could."

"We can't blame you," John said. "This is all very helpful. I've just got one more question. You said they originally came in at nine in the morning. Do you remember what time they left?"

"Oh, they were gone by nine thirty. As I said, there wasn't much we could do and we were trying to rush them out of here as fast as we could."

❧

It was time to pay Franklin a visit.

"I've got a bad feeling about this," Dick said.

John shifted the cruiser into drive. "Me too."

It was around one o'clock that Wednesday afternoon when they reached Franklin's house along Hosmer Pond in Camden. The

Buick was nowhere to be seen, but there was a new Corvette in the drive. It was curious to say the least. The wardens knocked on the front door several times before a man who met Sully's description of Franklin answered. He was about six foot two with bloodshot eyes, short dark hair askew from a night's sleep, and several days' worth of stubble on his face. Most notable were his thick, angry-looking eyebrows. The plain white t-shirt and blue plaid pajama pants he was wearing furthered the impression that he'd just woken up, but that didn't seem to slow him down from the beer can in his hand.

"What?" the man said by way of a greeting.

"Wayne Franklin?" John asked.

"Yeah. What d'ya want?"

"I'm Lieutenant Warden John Marsh, this here's District Warden Richard Hennessey. We're investigating a missing person's report. Would you mind letting us in to talk about any knowledge you may have of Ludger Belanger's whereabouts?"

"No point in it, never heard of the guy."

"Maybe you don't remember his name? We know you were in Washington yesterday hunting and that you picked up Ludger and his deer while he was dragging it out of the woods. We'd like to know where you dropped him off."

Franklin took a sip of his beer. "I don't know what you're talking about. I wasn't in Washington yesterday and I can't say I've ever been to Washington."

"Well, if you were out driving around looking for a place to hunt, maybe you didn't realize you were in Washington?"

"I don't hunt and I wasn't driving around picking hunters up yesterday."

"You don't hunt?"

"Nope."

"Do you have any firearms in the house?"

Franklin crossed his arms. "No."

"Do you own a forest green wool coat?"

"No."

"What about a pair of those fancy new insulated snowmobile boots? Perhaps a size 12?"

"How many questions do I have to answer before you get it? The answer's no—no, no, no."

"All right, end of subject," John said. "Here's the deal, Mr. Franklin. The reason we're here today is because we found a receipt on a woods road in Washington near where Ludger was reported to be hunting. The receipt was dated for yesterday and it was for radiator work on a Buick Special at Sully's garage in Union. The receipt had your name and address on it as the customer, and we know the car is registered in your name. This is a serious matter and I'm sure you want to help us out. I can see you're not fully dressed yet, so instead of standing here freezing with the door open, why don't you let us in so we can talk this through."

To John's surprise, Franklin nodded for them to come in. The house was a two-story ranch with an unfinished split stairwell at the entrance. Franklin led them upstairs to the kitchen, which also opened into the living room. Both rooms featured the same wallpaper with a bright orange, yellow, and brown floral pattern. The kitchen was ordinary, a white refrigerator, oven, dark-walnut stained cupboards, and a small, round wooden table, behind which a bay window provided a partial view of the pond.

Franklin pulled a chair out from the table and for a second John thought he was going to ask them to sit down. Instead, he held onto the top of the chair as a prop, in essence creating a barrier between him and the wardens.

"I bet I know how that receipt got there," Franklin said. "I sold that damned car last night at a bar in Rockland. Probably the guy

93

that bought it went hunting there this morning and it dropped out of the car."

"You sold the car last night?" John asked.

"That's right."

"To who?"

"Beats me."

"You don't know who you sold the car to?"

"Nope. I was pretty sauced up last night, don't remember much." Franklin took another sip of his beer as if to prove he was drinking the night before. "'Bout all I remember is he drove off with the car. Shit, I don't even know how much I sold it for."

"We noticed there's a nice new car in the driveway. Is it yours?"

"Yes. I bought it a few weeks back."

"What's wrong with it?"

"Nothing. That car's a beast."

"Let me get this straight. You've got a new Corvette, but you went out in a car that was on the verge of breaking down?"

"Yeah, well, I was trying to sell it."

"Did you tell the man who bought it that the car had radiator issues?"

Franklin smiled. "Like I said, I don't recall."

John had heard enough.

"Mr. Franklin, do you really expect us to believe you've never been to Washington and that you sold your car last night to some guy you don't know?"

"Whether you believe it or not, that's what happened."

"You're lying. I know you're lying because I found the repair receipt under four inches of snow. Since the storm ended late yesterday afternoon, there's no way it could have been left there this morning. The receipt had several inches of snow under it, which means it was dropped sometime yesterday morning. I have an eyewitness who said you were at the garage yesterday morning wearing hunting garb and that you left around 9:30. This would have given you plenty of time to get to Washington and lose the receipt yourself. Now, I suggest you start coming clean with us because there are two ways we can do this from here. The easy way is for you to let us take a look around. We want to see your hunting clothes and any firearms you have in the house. If you don't cooperate, Warden Hennessey will go get a search warrant while I make myself comfortable at your kitchen table until he returns. So what's it going to be? Truth or dare?"

Franklin furrowed his thick brows and stared at John. Never one to back down from confrontation, John returned the glare. There was no telling what Franklin was thinking behind his bloodshot, dark-brown eyes. An uneasy feeling overcame John.

"Yeah," Franklin finally said. "I was at the garage yesterday morning and I went hunting in Washington afterward. We drove down the road you talked about."

"Why didn't you tell us that before?"

"I don't like cops. They're always getting me into trouble for something."

"I wonder why that is." John couldn't help himself, but he also knew not to antagonize Franklin any further. "Did you pick up Ludger Belanger while he was dragging his deer out on the road?"

"No."

"Did you see him?"

"No"

"You drank a lot yesterday. Is it possible you don't remember?"

"I'm telling you, I've never seen the guy."

"And you didn't pick up the deer?"

"I wish I did, but there's never been a deer in that car while I've owned it."

"We can tell from the tracks that you guys drove in before Ludger had reached the road, and then were on your way back out after he'd started down the road. How do you explain that your car stopped and both you and a passenger got out at the exact place where Ludger's drag trail ends?"

"We saw his tracks along the road, and we thought we were going to meet him, but then we reached that spot where someone else had driven in and picked him up. We were curious and I had to take a leak so we got out to have a look. As far as we could tell it was a good-size buck. That got us going on pretty good—you know how hunters do, what a lucky son of a bitch he was. We hadn't seen anything for ages. From what I remember, we hung out there for a bit, drank a beer, and smoked a cigarette. Ludger and whoever else was long gone by the time we reached the end of the road."

"So you're saying there was a second vehicle?" Dick asked.

"Yep."

"Funny," Dick said. "We didn't see any other car tracks."

"That's probably because I drove over them."

"And you never saw the other vehicle?"

"Nope."

John didn't believe the second car story. If that were true, they would have found a second set of turnaround marks somewhere on the road. It wasn't worth pressing Franklin anymore. The way they were going, he might even have told them that the second car must have backed out the entire length of the road.

"Who was the passenger in your car?" John asked.

"My buddy Cole."

"Does Cole have a last name?"

"Daniels."

"How do you know Cole?"

"We hang out together at the VFW in Rockland."

"Is Cole handicapped?"

"He's got a bum right leg from getting shot in 'Nam."

"Alright. We're going to need to see your hunting gear—boots, clothes, and gun."

"They're all downstairs."

"Is anyone else home?"

"No."

"Okay, please take Warden Hennessey downstairs and show him your gear. If you don't mind, may I use your bathroom? It's been a long night and all the coffee today is catching up with me."

"No problem," Franklin said. "It's this way." He led them down a hallway and pointed out the bathroom. John went in and closed the door. He could still hear the hollow thudding of Dick's boots on the front plywood staircase. Once he'd finished his business, John returned to the kitchen, about to sit at the table, when a box caught his eye. The whole time they were interviewing Franklin, there was a box of Federal buckshot, 12-gauge, double-aught, on the table alongside a hunting knife. He peeked inside the box and there was a shell missing. The knife was unsheathed and clean, but it got him thinking. If there was a knife on the kitchen table. . . . John made his way to the refrigerator and grabbed ahold of the freezer door handle.

He hesitated, listening. The murmur of Dick and Franklin's conversation downstairs was barely audible.

John opened the door. Inside were stacks of small packages wrapped in white freezer paper. He squeezed one of the packages and felt the paper give in to his pressure. They weren't frozen.

The sound of Dick's boots coming back up the stairs sent John scurrying to sit at the table.

"He's shown me all there is to see," Dick said. John could tell by the tone in his voice that Dick was trying to get them out of there.

Equally anxious to hear Dick's report and share his bit of news, John took his cue and stood up from the table.

"Oh," John said to Franklin. "I forgot to ask. Have you had any luck hunting this year?"

"I'd expect a couple wardens to know better," Franklin said. "Don't you know there aren't any more deer in this county? That lucky Belanger guy must have got the only one."

"Yes, I've heard that." John thanked Franklin for his cooperation and they were on their way.

"So, what'd you see," John asked once they were back in the cruiser and on the road.

"Well," Dick said. "He showed me his boots, the jacket, and a pair of wool pants he said he'd worn Tuesday. Both the jacket and pants were hanging near his wood furnace to dry. He'd already washed them and I couldn't find any trace of blood or deer hair. The shotgun was on a counter along with a cleaning kit. It had already been wiped, oiled—the works. I did see, however, a hacksaw that had tissue residue on it."

"Deer or human?"

"Hard to say, but there was something else."

"What?"

"There's a room down there we weren't able to get into. It has a wooden door with a padlock on it. Franklin claims he never goes in there and doesn't even know what's in there. Said he was given the combination to the lock when he bought the place but lost it."

"Like hell," John said.

"That's what I thought. We have to get into that room."

"Getting a warrant shouldn't be an issue. This guy's filthy."

"I saw the knife and package of buckshot on the table when we came back up. Was that there the whole time?"

"It was. Surprised me too. The knife was clean, but the box had one shell missing." John held his breath for a moment, unsure how Dick would respond to what he had to say next. "I also found this," he said as he unzipped his coat, reached into his breast pocket, and handed Dick a package of deer meat he'd removed from Franklin's freezer.

"John—" Dick looked as though his eyes were going to pop out of his head.

"You don't have to say it," John said. "Right now I don't care if this won't be admissible in court. Charging him with illegal possession of deer meat is the furthest thing from my mind. There's a young lady whose husband has been missing for over a day and three young girls that want to know when daddy is coming home. If getting this meat into the lab can help lead us to him, then you can be damn sure that's my priority. When this is all said and done, we'll have plenty to nail that son of a bitch."

Dick didn't argue. "It's not even frozen yet," he said as he filed it into an evidence bag.

"I know."

Several moments had passed before Dick asked the question they were both thinking.

"Do you think Ludger's still alive?"

John stared at the road ahead, watching the double yellow lines and the hardened patches of ice disappear under the cruiser. In his mind's eye, a possible scenario was beginning to unfold. Drunk off their asses and already in a foul mood from the car troubles, Franklin and his buddy Cole came across Ludger and his deer. They offered to help and lured Ludger into the car. God knows what happened next, but perhaps an argument ensued. There was a shotgun in the front seat and Ludger was unarmed.

It was hard to believe someone would get killed over a deer, but John had been in the department long enough to know it wasn't the first time, and, sadly, likely not the last. He didn't want to believe this was the case. He wanted to hear the relief in Linda's voice when told her husband would be coming home. But he had to face the facts: A lying drunk, a missing car, and a freezer full of fresh deer meat. Nothing had made sense to this point, but it was starting to add up.

"No," he said.

The wardens brought their suspicions of foul play to the State Police. The police agreed the case warranted additional resources from both branches, and they provided John and Dick with background information on Wayne Franklin and Cole Daniels. Both men were Vietnam veterans with Purple Hearts, which likely played into their friendship. Not much was known of Daniels's service, other than he was injured in the line of duty, but Franklin was a highly decorated Marine with a Silver Star to his name. He was lucky to be alive, having survived a grenade blast, and now had a metal plate in his head. Upon returning stateside, Franklin took to collecting on his disability pension and began amassing quite the non-meritorious rap sheet. Barroom boxing was his biggest and most common offense, to go along with two D.U.I. charges, and, for good measure, one booking of public urination. Franklin was married; Daniels was single and, as far as they could tell, lived alone.

"A trained killer that's all messed up and just doesn't give a damn," John said in summary of the two suspects to the group of wardens and police officers reviewing the case. No one argued the point.

The two agencies worked together to put a plan into action. The police spread the word to be on the lookout for Franklin's Buick to any car dealership within a hundred miles, and alerted UPS drivers, mail carriers, school bus drivers, and anyone else who frequently traveled the area.

John paired Earl Kelly with Warden Langdon Chandler, who was known for his keen tracking senses, and assigned them with retracing the Washington woods road to look for any sign of a second vehicle turning around. As they suspected, there was no second vehicle. Fortunately, the snow had held, enabling Kelly and Chandler to also drive any possible route between the Washington woods road, Sully's garage, and Franklin's house in Camden looking for any place a vehicle may have pulled off the road. Unfortunately, their extensive search of numerous logging roads and other retired paths returned no leads.

Snow analysis completed by the State Police team concluded that Franklin and Daniels encountered Belanger's tracks, or, more likely, Belanger himself, somewhere between 10:30 and 11:30 a.m. The timeline worked out for how long it would have taken Franklin to drive the thirteen miles from Sully's garage to the Washington woods road, and back to the garage with plenty of time for who-knows-what activity in between. Everyone working the case agreed Franklin and Daniels must have picked up Belanger. What they had to prove was that the two were responsible for Belanger's disappearance, and the freezer full of fresh deer meat, the hacksaw, and the mysterious locked room in Franklin's basement were all key pieces of evidence.

As John had guessed, procuring search warrants for both Franklin and Daniels's residences wasn't an issue. Two teams set out to execute the search warrants at the same time to prevent either suspect from tipping off the other. John and Dick, along with

State Police officers Greg Morton and Brian Blanchet, arrived at Franklin's house around 4 p.m. on Friday. To their surprise, cars were lined up on both sides of the road and the driveway was fully packed.

"I don't believe it," Dick said. "He's having a party. Is this guy a total fool?"

"Or a genius," John said. "Good way to cover up evidence."

"Oh, no. You don't think?"

A ruckus of blaring music and screaming voices could be heard inside the house, but nobody answered John's repeated pounding on the front door. After several failed attempts, he reared back and kicked-in the door. A woman descending the staircase fell backward onto the stairs.

"What the hell?" she yelled, momentarily preoccupied with the drink she'd spilled on herself. Then she looked up. "Oh shit, it's the cops."

"Where's Wayne Franklin?" John asked, more of a demand than a question.

The woman pointed downstairs.

"Let's split up," John said. "Dick and I will go downstairs. Greg and Brian go up."

The front basement room was shoulder-to-shoulder crowded and a haze of pot smoke permeated the air. John spotted Franklin sitting on a fold-out chair in the far corner. Franklin saw him coming and he quickly popped several pills into his mouth and chased them down with beer.

"What was that?" John asked.

"Happy pills," Franklin said with a devious smile. His head swayed as he tried to hold John's gaze.

The blaring music went silent, and officers Morton and Blanchet could be heard upstairs announcing the party was over.

"What about that?" John pointed at a fist-sized hole in the wall.

"That . . . that's where we hid the stuff."

"What stuff?"

Franklin shrugged his shoulders. "Stuff."

John pulled out his pocketknife and began cutting a square of sheetrock around the hole.

"What are you doing?" Franklin shouted. "You can't cut my wall."

"This search warrant says I can." John held it up for Franklin to see. Then he shined his flashlight into the new opening.

Looking back to Dick, John said, "There's nothing in here."

"Uh oh," Franklin said, nearly falling out of his seat, "we're out of stuff."

"John." Dick motioned with his head for them to conference on the other side of the room. Except for a few stragglers, the party had already cleared out.

"It's all gone," Dick said.

"What's gone?"

"You name it. The green coat, wool pants, snowmobile boots, shotgun, shells, hacksaw, knife—everything."

Without saying a word John rushed upstairs. A newspaper article on Ludger Belanger's disappearance had been cut out and taped to the freezer door. John gasped for breath as if he'd been sucker punched. He opened the door already knowing what he wasn't going to find inside.

Empty.

"We don't cook much," a woman said in a muffled voice.

John turned to find the woman who'd fallen on the stairwell sitting at the kitchen table with her head in her arms.

"The wife," Officer Blanchet said.

"Great. Two peas in a pod."

"Dick is asking for you downstairs. He's opening the back room."

John remembered Dick telling him about the padlocked door, and suddenly there was a glimmer of hope. Downstairs, Dick was standing at the wooden door. "The padlock," he said, "is facing out. I distinctly remember it being the other way around yesterday."

"That's curious."

"Especially since Franklin told me he'd lost the combination."

They cut the padlock. At first glance, the room appeared empty and the musty stench corroborated Franklin's story that he never went in there. A string hung from a light fixture in the center of the room. It actually worked, and the single bulb dimly illuminated the room.

"Looks like a new bulb," John said. "No dust."

"Come here," Dick said from the corner of the room. He was shining his flashlight on a countertop that was covered in a film of mold. There were imprints in the mold where something had been laid on the counter. "Does that look like a gun could have been set there to you?"

"Possibly. Not long enough to be the shotgun, but . . . " John studied the marks from end to end. "It's about right for a .30-30." Then John saw something else. "What's that?"

Dick saw it too and he shined his light on a small, flat, steel piece. "It looks like half of a v-notch sight," he said. "The type typically found on a .30-30."

"We're going to have to get that into the lab," John said.

Franklin was still sitting in the fold-out chair when they came back through. He lifted his beer in recognition of the wardens and took another sip.

"What did you do with everything?" John asked.

"I don't know what you're talking about," Franklin said.

"I think you do. Where's your hunting clothes and the shotgun?"

Franklin smiled. "I told you guys the last time you were here, I don't have any hunting gear in the house."

"You did," Dick said. "You showed it to me." Dick was keeping himself together, but John could tell he was boiling beneath the surface, wanting nothing more than to slug Franklin.

"Did I?" Franklin said, rhetorically. "I don't think so. Warden Marsh, did you see a gun or any clothes before?"

"No." Now John wanted to punch him. Franklin knew John had stayed upstairs and it was his word versus Dick's. John had seen the knife and shotgun shells, but it wasn't worth pushing the point because they had no evidence. "Why is that article taped to your freezer door?"

"You were accusing me of things—lots of things—so I wanted to know what the hell it was about." Franklin stopped swaying for a second and looked John in the eye. "I told you I don't trust cops. They're always out to get me."

"I've stopped wondering why that is," John said. "Sooner or later we're going to wipe that shit-eating grin off your face."

Franklin took another sip of beer. "Good luck with that."

For John, there was no masking his disappointment. He'd arrived at the residence with the full intention of leaving with Franklin in handcuffs, but other than the steel piece, all they could justify confiscating was an empty beer can for fingerprinting. Follow-up examination of the steel piece confirmed it was the broken right half of a v-sight consistent with the Winchester .30-30 model sold at the Sears, Roebuck & Company in Augusta, which was where Ludger Belanger's rifle had been bought. This evidence wasn't nearly enough to justify an arrest warrant because there was no way to prove that the piece had come from Belanger's gun.

To make matters worse, the second team that searched Daniels's residence at the same time also struck out. There were no hunting clothes or equipment of any kind on the premises, and Daniels stonewalled all interview attempts. He insisted that if he wasn't under arrest, he wasn't saying a damn thing.

This left John and everyone else in law enforcement with some hair-raising suspicions and two prime suspects, but no proof. It was pure frustration. John knew the investigation was far from over, but it was time for him to do the one thing he'd wanted to avoid all along.

◆～◆

Once again John found himself knocking on Linda Belanger's front door. This time, he was joined by Father Raymond Michaud, better known as Father Ray, from the Belanger's church. John had delivered death notices to families before, a reality of the job he, nor anyone else, enjoyed, but this was a devil of an entirely different pitchfork. Linda was sure to have questions and he lacked the answers she deserved. It was an ongoing investigation so the information he had couldn't be disclosed.

A woman who introduced herself as Linda's mother answered the door and led them into the family's living room. Linda was sitting on a sofa and she stood up to greet them, but upon seeing Father Ray, she immediately began shaking and fell back onto the couch.

"No," she said, sobbing. "No!"

"We have reason to believe . . ." John started to say as if he were reading from a script. He'd run the conversation through his mind a hundred times or more, but now he found himself without the words.

"He's not dead." Linda was rocking back and forth. "He's not."

"We have reason—"

"No!"

Father Ray sat beside Linda and took her hands into his. "It's good to have faith," he told her. "The wardens are doing their job, and at this point, Ludger hasn't been found dead or alive. It's John's responsibility to tell you they expect the worst when a person has been missing this long, but the Lord delivers miracles every day, and until we know one way or the other, you keep listening to your heart."

"Ludgie's not . . ." Linda stared at the floor, a steady stream of tears dripping from the tip of her nose. "I don't believe it . . . I . . . can't believe it."

Shortly after leaving the Belanger residence, John was informed that a forest green Buick Special was found on a residential road in Northport, east of Route 1. The VIN number matched that of the Buick registered to Wayne Franklin, and the location was roughly a twenty-minute drive from his Camden home.

John arrived on the scene a little after dusk. "Do you have a wrecker coming to impound the vehicle?" he asked Stephen Lambert, the State Police officer controlling the scene.

Lambert looked concerned. "John, on what grounds can we impound it? The car is parked legally and it's someone's private property. For all we know it was sold and parked here."

"Let's see," John said. He shined his flashlight into the back window. "I'll be damned," he muttered to himself. The rear seat, floor mats, and headliner were all missing. John went to the back of the car and popped open the trunk. A pungent, unmistakable odor of Lestoil wafted out. The trunk floor mat had been removed, as had the spare tire and any accessories that may have been in the tire well. "This guy's one foul, slippery fish," he whispered. John shined his flashlight around, stopping it when a familiar sight on the inside of the trunk lid caught his eye. "But you didn't catch everything."

"We've got our cause," John announced to Lambert. "I've found a deer hair. We can pinch him for instrumentalities of transporting an unlawful deer. I've got Franklin on record saying there's never been a deer in the car."

The deer hair wasn't the big find they were hoping to get out of the Buick, but it was a start, and it was enough to get the car impounded. The following day, John and Dick arrived together at the State Police barracks while a forensics team was casing the vehicle. The car was up on a lift and the officers were checking the underside when the wardens entered the garage.

"I'm sorry to say," one of the officers said to the wardens, "the car has been totally cleaned. These guys knew what they were doing. Other than the deer hair you recovered, we haven't found any prints, fluids, hairs—nothing." They lowered the car to the ground. "It's spotless."

"You mind if we take a peek?" John asked.

"Help yourself," the officer said. "We're done with it."

John and Dick both went straight to the trunk and began nosing around. The Lestoil smell was still strong, and everything had a newly cleaned shine. The trunk was empty except for the spare tire and jack.

"What's that?" Dick asked.

"What?"

Dick pointed to the spare tire wheel well. "Looks like a buckshot pellet to me."

John leaned in to take a closer look. "I think you're right."

The forensic officers were milling around in the back of the garage and John yelled for them to return. After taking a few photos and documenting where the pellet was found, the main officer who'd spoken to them before reached in and removed it with a pair of tweezers.

"Look at that," the officer said, as he held the pellet up for John to see. There was what appeared to be a human beard hair hanging from the pellet.

John's mind was off to the races. When he first interviewed Linda, she'd told him Ludger had a goatee. "What he can grow, anyway," she'd said, almost apologetically. "It doesn't fully connect." For the next few weeks, John held out hope that they'd finally discovered the key piece of evidence to connect Ludger with Franklin's Buick.

The results from the FBI lab in Washington, D.C. came back inconclusive. They weren't able to match it to either Belanger, Franklin, or Daniels.

This dead end didn't dissuade either agency from the investigation. Everyone involved subscribed to the adage that where there's smoke, there's fire, and if anything, finding the buckshot pellet *in* the Buick only fueled their belief that Franklin and Daniels had lit the match. The burden of proof, however, was on the agencies, and with each lead that didn't pan out, it grew more and more burdensome. The following spring, the Warden Service filled a local hotel with personnel for a week to conduct an extensive search of the area. The event was without precedent and many of the wardens involved were there as volunteers. The community came to their aid in full force with members of the Rod and Gun Club helping with the search; the hotel, closed for the winter, opened early and provided a discount rate; stores donated food and meals were served courtesy of the local Grange. The wardens and volunteers combed the woods with cadaver dogs; search planes circled the area looking for clusters of crows that could indicate the location of a decomposing body; and divers were sent to the area's numerous quarries, ponds, lakes, and rivers.

No new evidence was found.

Leads continued to trickle in and the agencies investigated all of them, from testing a car-seat spring found at the Union dump, to draining a farmer's pond and uncovering only muck. A break came when a man named Chris went to the police claiming he'd been told the Belanger story while partying with Daniels. According to Chris's account, Franklin and Daniels lured Belanger into the car with the intent of stealing his deer. When Franklin told Belanger they were keeping the deer as their shipping and handling fee, Belanger balked. He said he needed to feed his family and asked to be let out of the car. That's when Daniels lowered the shotgun barrel over the seat and pulled the trigger. Chris didn't ask what happened to the body. He and Daniels were drinking at the time and he was afraid of what Daniels might do to him. "It was all messed up," he'd told police.

Everyone knew Chris's account wasn't enough to prosecute. While he relayed facts of the case that weren't public knowledge, even a lousy defense attorney would have a field day with a substance-induced confession. What Chris gave them was hope. Around the same time, Daniels was once again afoul of the law, arrested and imprisoned for possession of stolen property, his drug addiction having grown to the point where it couldn't be supported by disability checks alone. The warden at the Maine State Prison in Thomaston cut an early-release deal with one of the inmates, provided the snitch could procure information from Daniels on the Belanger disappearance. Daniels, however, was true to his original statement that he wasn't saying a damn thing. Making matters worse, Chris died shortly after that of a drug overdose.

The watchful eye of the law also stayed trained on Wayne Franklin. The military sent two undercover officers to hang out at the VFW in Rockland. They became fast friends with Franklin, but despite his being a functional alcoholic with a severe drug addiction, all part and parcel of his notoriously volatile nature, they weren't able to get the slightest bit of information from him.

Then, on July 29, 1976, seven months after the disappearance of Ludger Belanger, Wayne Franklin finally slipped up, giving hope the case would be solved.

John was in his Augusta office reviewing paperwork when he received a call from Greg Morton.

"You're not gonna believe this," Greg said. "Remember your old friend Wayne Franklin?"

"How could I forget?"

"He's blown up his house in Camden."

"Are you serious?"

"I am. It appears to be an attempt at insurance fraud. He filled a bunch of washtubs with gasoline and lit a candle wick as a fuse. Franklin had a round-trip ticket from Bangor airport to Orlando. He wasn't scheduled to return for a week, so it's pretty obvious he was trying to make it look like he wasn't home when the explosion occurred. Trouble for him is he never made it off the premises. The house must have been so filled with fumes that something—who knows, maybe the refrigerator—triggered the explosion before he got out. The blast shot him straight through the kitchen window."

"You're right, I don't believe it. Is he dead?"

"Not yet. They've flown him to a military burn center in San Antonio, but they don't expect him to last long. I have a detective going to Texas to get a dying declaration."

"Unbelievable. Please let me know as soon as you know anything more."

"I will."

"I mean it, call anytime, day or night."

"Don't worry, John, I know how important this one is to you. We've both come a long way with it. It'll be nice to finally put it to rest."

John wasn't able to sleep that night. He'd stayed in touch with Linda since the incident, and he wanted to tell her they may soon be able to locate Ludger's remains. But he knew better. After the long list of dead-end leads they endured throughout the case, he'd made a promise with himself to not get her heart set on closure until they knew for sure. So he waited. The following day, he occupied his mind with busy work, following up with field wardens on their various cases, anything to keep from just sitting at his desk and become prey to his thoughts. The call came around mid-afternoon.

"John, I'm sorry," Greg said. "Franklin passed before we could get to him."

John sighed.

"We tried," Greg said.

"This isn't over," John said. "I don't know if it ever will be."

CHAPTER NINE

Eyes in the Sky

WARDEN PILOT GARY DUMOND PUSHED ON THE THROTTLE AND his Piper Super Cub lifted off the water. It didn't matter how many years he'd been flying, or how many flights he'd made, that feeling of being suddenly suspended in air, no longer connected to the ground, never got old. Flying was in Gary's blood, every bit a part of his DNA as his brown hair and blue eyes.

Gary's father had been a bush pilot with his own flight service. From as early as he could remember, Gary had been flying with his dad, and in those days, it wasn't uncommon for his father to join the wardens at the Eagle Lake plane base for a game of cards. Gary tagged along, of course, mesmerized by the warden pilots' tales of search and rescue. When sitting around the card table sunk into boredom, he'd sneak into one of the planes, climb into the pilot's seat, don the headset, and grip the throttle. His imaginative flying extended beyond liftoff as he scanned the landscape for lost hunters. It was a phase he never outgrew. As a teenager, Gary sometimes rode his bike the twelve miles to Eagle Lake to see warden pilot Dick Varney. If Dick was out, Gary waited for hours on end for his plane to splash down on the lake so he could hear about Dick's latest adventure—gut-wrenching tales of searching for missing people in northern Maine's vast backcountry, some on the verge of death when found. In Gary's eyes, Dick was a hero.

By the time Gary was a senior in high school, the reality of becoming a warden pilot was all too clear. To this point, there had only been ten pilots in the history of the Warden Service, and Gary knew six of them. Once hired, warden pilots tended to stay on the job until retirement, or otherwise indisposed through tragedy. Quite simply: He may never have the opportunity to become a warden pilot; however, this didn't dissuade Gary from wanting to be a pilot altogether. The day he saw an Army ad in *Flying Magazine* with the headline, "High School to Flight School," Gary called. This moment set in motion a career path that soon found him manning helicopters in Vietnam war zones at nineteen years old.

Airborne, Gary checked his instruments and set his course. It was the last week of hunting season in the fall of 1979. He'd received the call in the wee hours of the morning. A Canadian hunter hadn't come out of the woods the afternoon before in an area of northwestern Maine known as Big Bog. Snow had started falling during the day, likely causing the hunter to get disoriented, and it continued overnight, amassing a foot of accumulation. Gary left his station in Old Town before dawn, knowing it was a fine line in these conditions between search and rescue, and search and recovery. He typically liked to arrive while it was still dark in case the lost person had lit a fire, making it easier to see the embers. With the snowfall, there wasn't much point in this strategy, so Gary timed his hour-and-a-half flight to reach Big Bog at daybreak.

As darkness clocked out and daylight took over, Gary found himself enshrouded in a sea of gray. The lack of visibility at higher altitudes wasn't a concern because he could rely on the plane's instruments to navigate. The question was going to be how low he'd have to fly at Big Bog to get under the cloud cover and see the ground. The bigger issue was all the moisture lingering in the fog. By the time Gary reached Big Bog and local Warden Curt Daigle welcomed his pair of eyes in the sky over the radio, a fair amount of ice had already accumulated on the propeller and wings, and it was beginning to freeze up the windows. If Gary were to be their eyes, it wouldn't be long before his eyelids were half shut.

"What's our position of last seen?" Gary asked.

Curt relayed coordinates. "It's a hardwood ridge. Our guy split from his party near an old maple sugar shack that's up there."

Gary flew over the ridge and spotted the weathered-gray shack. Typically, he'd be able to see tracks in the snow, but the fresh accumulation was concealing all but the most recent footprints, of which he didn't see any. Knowing the man was last seen near the shack was helpful, but there were no guarantees he would be anywhere near it. The hunter had been missing for approximately twelve hours; if he was moving during the night and he averaged a mile per hour, he could be twelve miles from the shack in any direction. Take into consideration any travel he did during the previous day, and it wasn't out of the question that the man could be seventeen or eighteen miles from the shack. This meant they had a possible search area of approximately 113 miles. Given the conditions, the odds of a quick rescue were stacked against the lost hunter, and with each minute that passed, the realities of hypothermia heightened.

"Do we know what he's wearing?" Gary said into the radio. On a good day, he could see someone dressed in hunter orange from ten miles away, but this wasn't a good day. The fog ceiling was lowering, requiring Gary to fly into the clouds to clear the bigger hills.

"We're not sure," Curt responded. "I'm not getting a straight answer from his buddies. Their English is just as bad as my French."

"Wonderful."

They were only eight miles from Quebec, and it was common practice for Canadian hunters to cross the border and get a Maine hunting license. Without any real travel, it afforded them the opportunity to double their bag limit on deer for the season.

Gary's plane had four hours of flight time per tank of fuel, and he carried reserves for three hours more. Counting the hour and a half flight to reach the search area, he now had a little under two hours before he'd have to land on a body of water to refuel. At this time of year that meant the larger lakes, because the smaller ponds were already freezing. Gary scanned the landscape looking for anything that seemed out of place. The exercise of searching for hunters wasn't much different than hunting. The irony that he began his pilot career peering into the woods for men with guns to avoid being shot at, and now he was trying to rescue them, wasn't lost upon Gary.

The ice was continuing to build on the plane's windows, further limiting his view. One of the most frustrating aspects of the job was knowing there was someone on the ground who was likely scared, half frozen, and suffering, and this person could easily hear him coming and see his bright yellow plane for miles, but he couldn't see them. Gary imagined their fear and frustration, left to wonder if they'd ever be found. He called it the funnel effect. Those on the ground were looking up through the wide part of the funnel, while the realities of the Piper Cub's tiny windows, wings, long nose, and propeller, left him with the small hole at the bottom of the funnel to see through.

The hunter orange law had been a game changer, making it much easier to spot people. In one case, Gary and warden pilot

Jim Welch spent a full day combined searching for a lost hunter. It wasn't until it had started snowing and was close to getting dark that Gary saw something glowing on the horizon, a good twelve miles from the search area. Low and behold, it was their orange-clad missing person. Not everyone enters the woods in bright colors, of course, and even if they do it's still important for a lost person to aid their rescue. Something as simple as waving at the plane could help catch his eye. In his career, he's found over 200 people, many of whom did something to get his attention, including the woman he once spotted waving a piece of white clothing in the air, which upon closer inspection, turned out to be her bra. Those who lit fires were always easy to find, and some took it to extremes. One man torched an entire bog while another set a cluster of birch trees ablaze.

The ice buildup on the plane was posing more issues than visibility. It added weight and affected airflow over the wings, forcing Gary to fly with less-tight turns and more coasting, which ultimately caused the plane to go faster. Plus, the more the plane coasted, the greater the risk of the engine stalling. In a normal search, Gary would fly at 500 to 1,000 feet above ground, but the low cloud cover was forcing him to stay around 200 feet above the trees. Altogether, it was a recipe for disaster.

In hazardous situations, it's the warden pilot's responsibility to ground the plane, but it's also the pilot's discretion to determine what's too dangerous to fly. And that's the rub. At what point does a person whose job description is search and rescue value their life over another's? It's a gray area that can become more obscure when the search involves women and children. Dick had taught Gary to always have an out, and in this case, his plan was to fly the plane fifteen miles east to where he could land on an open lake. What's debatable is whether the safety net of an out makes the pilot safer or provides a false sense of security. Gary, of all people, needn't be reminded of the risks. It's how he got the job with the Warden Service in the first place.

When the Vietnam War had started to wind down, Gary was offered early leave and he took it. Back in Maine, he landed a job as a pilot for the Forest Service. In this role, he became the first person in the state to fly a helicopter with a water bucket over forest fires. As exciting as that was, it wasn't his dream job, which, he unfortunately didn't have to wait long to get. Tragedy struck the Warden Service: Dick perished in a crash. Already employed as a pilot by the State of Maine, as well as a known supporter of the Warden Service, Gary earned the position. And so it was that he assumed the post of the man he'd so often shadowed and admired as a child. Sometimes, in the close-knit warden community, that's exactly how it goes.

<hr />

"Find a space, show your face," Gary said aloud to himself, reciting the mantra they so often promoted in public relations. It had been an hour since he'd arrived over the Big Bog wilderness area, and Gary had yet to see any sign of the lost hunter. Likewise, the wardens on the ground hadn't had any luck, occasionally firing location shots in hopes of a response. Gary was beginning to think the search might not have a happy ending. It reminded him of the time he spotted a hunter who had suffered a heart attack. The man was sitting against a tree cradling his gun as if he'd taken a nap.

The odds of seeing anything in these conditions were nearing non-existent. The front windshield was now completely frozen over and Gary knew he had to land the plane. The air would be warmer down at the lake and the ice would melt, enabling him to return to the search in about an hour. Gary looked out the side window as he spoke into the radio to tell the wardens on the ground he had to abort. In that instant, he saw a face looking up at him and his words became jumbled.

"Come again," Curt said, "we didn't copy."

The man was standing on an old tote road, staring up at the plane. He made no attempt to flag the plane down, nor was he wearing so much as a stitch of orange.

"I think I see our guy," Gary said. "Ask his buddies again if he's wearing orange."

It took a minute for Curt to respond. "No, he's not."

"Okay, this has got to be our guy. He's only about a half mile from you."

"Seriously?"

"Yes. It's as if he doesn't want to be found."

"He's probably afraid of getting busted without his orange, so instead, he's risking his life. Some people. . . ."

"That'd be my guess. He's also on a tote road, so he probably thinks he can make it. Look, my plane is covered in ice, I need to land immediately. I'll make a pass over him and gun the engine so you can get his location." After doing this, Gary checked in. "Got it?"

"I think so, can you make one more pass to confirm?"

"Just one."

On the second pass, Curt confirmed they were all set. "Get out of here. Safe landing."

"Ten-four."

Gary landed on nearby Seboomook Lake with a sigh of relief. It didn't take long for the ice on the plane to melt, and after fueling up, Gary was able to make the flight back to Old Town. As for the hunter, he was in the early stages of hypothermia when the wardens got to him; his overnight ordeal and reluctance to aid the search ultimately cost him several fingers and toes to frostbite.

He was lucky.

CHAPTER TEN

Dead Man Walking

MARTIN SAVAGE SAT DOWN AT THE KITCHEN TABLE AND BEGAN to think about taking off his boots. After a long day patrolling Mooselookmeguntic Lake in a sixteen-foot boat with a nearly useless five-horsepower motor, there was no point rushing now. This moment was his unwind time, and he hadn't so much as bothered to turn on the overhead light. It was overcast outside, and the house was as dark as dark can be. Most of the day had been sunny and unseasonably hot for mid-September, but a front was moving in, and the temperatures were plummeting into the forties. The walls of his old house creaked as the chill from a breeze billowed open the window curtains.

The sound reminded him to check on his daughter and bring her an extra blanket. He leaned forward and began to pluck at his boot laces. His back protested the motion, a stiffness that was mostly all for naught. It had been a slow day on the lake, his five-horsepower motor giving anyone afoul of the law ample time to conceal their behavior before he could reach them. The only person he nabbed was a woman in a canoe who was fishing without a license. She swore up and down that she didn't know she needed one, and Martin believed her. Had she been fishing with a kid, he probably would have let her off with a warning. But the woman was with her husband, and he remained silent in the back of the canoe while she pleaded her ignorance, a telltale sign that he knew better. It was too bad she was the one he had to write up.

Martin coaxed off his boots and socks and set his bare feet on the cold, wooden floor. And then the phone rang. He checked his watch; it was almost 11 p.m.

"Speaking," Martin said to the dispatcher, his end of the conversation further consisting of "Uh-huh . . . Okay . . . I see . . . I'll be right there."

Martin sat down again to put his boots back on; this time, his actions had a purpose.

"Is everything okay?" he heard his wife ask. Martin looked up to see her standing near the doorframe with an afghan wrapped around her.

"Some fool shot a deer in someone's front yard," he told her. "I've got to check it out. I don't know how late I'll be, probably all night. You should go back to bed."

"Have you eaten?" she asked. "There's meatloaf in the fridge."

"I had something," he said, avoiding the real answer.

"Be careful."

"You know it."

"I do. That's why I worry."

Martin smiled. "Well then, I guess you know me."

"Be careful."

"You know it."

She retreated down the hall muttering something about him being impossible.

The deer had been shot at an old farmhouse on Route 16 in the village of Wilsons Mills. When Martin arrived on the scene, he found the deer, a doe, dead in a flower bed at the front of the house. There was blood splatter on the white clapboards along with a red smear where the deer collapsed against the house. The family, understandably, was still shaken up.

"The kids were in bed and we were watching the news in that room there," the wife explained, pointing to the smear. "We heard a car pass by and then—bang!" She waved her hands frantically at her side and then clapped them over her nose and mouth. "We could have been shot!"

"It obviously scared us," her husband said, "but I just assumed the car had backfired. Then there were more shots and the thump of the deer against the house."

"How many shots were fired?" Martin asked.

"I counted three," the husband said, "but it all happened so fast, I'm not positive about that. I think the deer was off to the side of the house when they fired the first shot and then ran in front."

"Did you see anyone?"

"No. I ran into the kitchen to look out the window from there, and all I saw were the cars."

"How many cars?"

"There were two sedans. I don't know the make, and I'm sorry, I can't even tell you the color."

"It's okay," Martin said. "Which way did they go?"

"East toward Rangeley."

"Alright, I'm on it. I doubt they'll come back, but get your family inside and lock the doors and windows just in case. Please don't touch the deer or the blood, we'll get another officer out here to collect evidence soon."

Martin sped toward Rangeley as fast as he could in his department truck, but Route 16 out of Wilsons Mills in 1966 was a narrow obstacle course of hills, sharp turns, frost-heave damage, and potholes. It took a while, but Martin eventually caught up to a vehicle with Quebec plates near Cupsuptic Lake and pulled it over. He shined his flashlight inside the car as he approached it on foot and counted three men in the vehicle—two in front, one in the back.

"Bonjour," the driver said.

"Where are you coming from?" Martin asked, skipping the pleasantries.

The driver launched into a quick-tongued, long-winded explanation in French.

Martin cut him off. "In English."

"Eh. . .Farmington Fair," the driver said.

The driver seemed relatively sober, but the two passengers had a glazed-over look and Martin could smell alcohol.

"You're heading in the wrong direction to be coming from Farmington," Martin said.

The driver shrugged. "Miss turn."

Martin ordered the three men out of the vehicle and patted them down. The driver had a large pocket knife, but none of them were concealing any firearms. He then had them open the trunk. All that was inside was the spare tire and a pair of chest-high waders. Martin searched the waders to make sure a gun hadn't been hidden inside. He then checked the glove compartment and under the seats. Nothing but trash, empty beer cans, and a half-eaten candy apple, the latter of which corroborated their story of having been at the fair.

"Where's the other car?" Martin asked the men.

"*Quelle voiture?*" the man who had been sitting in the back said.

"In English," Martin said. "The other car you were following, where is it?"

"*Je ne sais pas,*" the driver started to say before catching himself. "No car."

"You weren't caravanning with another car of people tonight?"

"No," the driver said.

Martin shook his head in disbelief. It was too much of a coincidence for these men to be drinking and cruising around this late at night in the middle of nowhere—especially traveling in the wrong direction—for them to have not been involved in the incident. He didn't have anything to hold them on, and he was wasting time trying to talk to them. He had no choice but to let them go. Without waiting to see what they would do, Martin jumped into his truck and sped onto Route 16 toward Rangeley. In his rearview he saw the Canadians turn their car around and head in the opposite direction.

At least, Martin now had something more to go on—he was looking for a sedan with Quebec plates. Working a district on the Canada border, he was no stranger to pinching Canadians who'd run afoul of Maine's fish and game laws. In fact, he'd once nabbed four fishermen who were in possession of 148 trout on a five-fish-per-person limit. As egregious as that incident had been, this situation was life threatening, and Martin was coming to the sober realization that the shooter was likely long gone. Maybe, just maybe, the other car will pull over to wait for their friends. He could only hope.

As Martin approached the Kennebago River bridge, he saw light from an oncoming vehicle shining on the trees ahead. He gripped the steering wheel tight with anticipation. Perhaps the people in the other car were coming back to check on their friends? Martin crossed the bridge and parked his truck perpendicular in the middle of the road to prevent the vehicle from passing. The oncoming car came around the bend and into sight. Martin stood in front of his truck and waved his heavy flashlight in the air. The vehicle began to slow down as it approached the roadblock. This was the car, Martin could feel it. Sure enough, as it got close, he could see it was a silver, four-door Pontiac Tempest with Quebec plates.

The vehicle coasted slowly toward Martin. Then the Pontiac suddenly accelerated onto the shoulder in an attempt to go around his truck. Martin threw his flashlight at the car. There was a loud crack as it bounced off the windshield and went out. The car fishtailed in the grass at the top of a steep bank as Martin ran to it yelling for the driver to stop. He reached inside the open car window and hooked his arm on the driver's door. The next thing Martin knew he was being dragged alongside the car as it swerved onto the bridge and accelerated. He held on for dear life, his boots scraping the pavement—this was the exact type of situation his wife was worried about.

With his free hand, Martin grabbed his pistol and aimed it at the front tire. His first shot ricocheted off the tire and clanked the car's underside. A woman in the back seat started yelling in bursts of high-pitched, hysterical shrieks. Martin's second shot rattled around inside the wheel well.

While both bullets failed to pierce the tire, the gunshots were enough to convince the driver to stop. Martin was able to regain his footing and do a quick headcount. There were three men in the vehicle, plus the woman who was sitting behind the front passenger seat, her shrieks having now evolved into a sobbing wail. The driver had a revolver in his lap, and upon his recognition that Martin saw the gun, he handed it to the man in the front passenger seat. Martin scampered around the front of the car to disarm the passenger, who turned it into a game of hot potato, quickly handing the gun back to the driver. Going with his momentum, Martin ran around the back of the car and pointed his pistol at the driver as he got to the window.

"Give me the gun," Martin demanded.

Just then, he felt cold steel being pressed into the back of his head. There was no need to look, he knew exactly what it was.

"I don't think so," a man behind him said. "You drop it."

The driver slid his hand down Martin's arm and pried the pistol away from him. It had all happened so fast, Martin didn't realize the man in the back seat was getting out of the car behind him with a rifle. Now all three men were out, and they each had a gun. The driver and the front-seat passenger went in front of the idling car to inspect the windshield, which Martin could see had spider-web fracturing where the flashlight hit, along with a large crack running the full width.

The man with the rifle said something in French to the woman in the back seat. She continued to sob, and as far as Martin could tell she was being told to stay put.

"Move," the man with the rifle said to Martin. "To the truck." He pressed the barrel into Martin's back and gave him a push. As frightening as this was, Martin found the conversation the men were having equally troubling. He couldn't tell what they were saying, but Martin expected some conflict and uncertainty between them, and there was too much head nodding for his liking. These guys were plotting, and whatever they were saying, they appeared to be in agreement.

When they got to the truck, the man who had been driving the car went into the cab to retrieve Martin's keys while the front-seat passenger opened the hood. The two proceeded to work at a frenzied pace, cutting out whatever wires and hoses they could, determined to make sure they couldn't be followed. This gave Martin a glimmer of hope that they may be leaving him behind, but then the man with the rifle was once again pushing him in the back.

"Let's go," he said.

"Where to?" Martin asked.

"To the car. We're going for a ride."

The man's words, *we're going for a ride*, echoed in Martin's thoughts as he started back toward the car. It was too dark to see any details with clarity, which prevented him from getting a good look at the man with the rifle; however, the other two had made the mistake of walking in front of the car to inspect the windshield. With the headlights shining on them, Martin could see they were both average height with broad shoulders, full beards, and scraggly brown hair. The driver was wearing a flannel shirt while the front-seat passenger, despite the plummeting temperatures, was in a tank-top. They both had work boots on, adding to their stereotypical lumberjack appearance, which meant they likely worked in one of the logging outfits near the border. Martin could identify them, knew their vehicle make and model, not to mention the easy-to-spot windshield spider web, and had a good idea of where to start looking—finding these men after this incident was a near certainty. Whether they realized this or not, they had to know kidnapping a warden at gunpoint wasn't something they'd get away with, unless. . . .

The two men who'd dismembered the truck, threw the keys, hoses, and wires over the side of the bridge. It was quiet enough to hear the splashing below. Martin didn't realize he'd stopped to listen, but the man with the rifle did, pushing it deeper into his back.

We're going for a ride.

People often referred to Martin's district as God's country, but if he got in the car, there was no doubt it was about to become his personal hell. The area had a surplus of logging roads and little-used dirt paths, providing an abundance of options for escaping what passed as civilization around these parts. These were places where nary a soul would hear a gunshot fired in the middle of the night. The deepest of woods where a discarded body might never be found.

Martin looked ahead to the car.

He might as well climb into his own coffin.

He thought of his wife and daughter, safe and sound in their beds, completely unaware of his situation. Yes, they worried, but they were also accustomed to him coming home. That wouldn't be the case tonight. Would they ever learn what happened to him? Or forever live with the burden of uncertainty?

He was quite literally a dead man walking. Nothing left to lose.

And then it clicked.

Martin started running.

With each step, he expected to hear the explosion of gunfire.

Martin jumped off the edge of the bridge. It was only a ten-foot drop, but he seemed to hang in the air forever—an easy target.

Then he hit the ground. His legs gave way and his body tumbled head-first down the bank. Bushes scratched his face and neck. When he stopped rolling, Martin was at the edge of a large culvert. He crawled inside upon the cold river rocks that had been washed up during the spring surge. He lay motionless, trying to hold his breath, afraid the sound of his rapid breathing was going to reveal his location. There was yelling coming from both sides of the bridge above, but the men didn't have a light and it was too dark to see this far down. Eventually, their voices disappeared, followed by the slamming of car doors and the roar of the engine accelerating down the road.

Martin continued to stay where he was hidden in case the fleeing car was a ruse. He was accustomed to waiting in the dark of night, and there was no point rushing now. It was the better part of an hour before he crawled out of the culvert and crept into the woods. It wouldn't be safe for him to walk along the road, so he made his way through the forest to some camps along Cupsuptic Lake. There he was able to wake a camp owner and access a telephone.

The following morning, Martin returned home to take a shower and change his clothes. His wife caught him in the kitchen as he was putting on his boots.

"How was your night?" she asked.

"Oh, you know, some fools shot a deer in someone's front yard. I went after them. The usual."

"I got a call this morning from Jack Shaw. It didn't sound like the usual."

"It's really no big deal."

She rolled her eyes. "And you wonder why I worry?"

"It's no wonder," he admitted.

"Where are you off to now? Aren't you going to get some sleep first?"

"I wish I could, I really do, but these fools drove through the border crossing and got the Mounties on their tails early this morning before we could send word on what they'd done here. The good news is they're in custody, but I have to appear in Canadian court today to report on their actions last night and get them sent to Farmington for trial here."

Martin finished tying his laces and leaned back in the chair. His back was still sore from the previous day. "Don't worry, dear, I'll sleep tonight. We'll take the phone off the hook to make sure of it."

CHAPTER ELEVEN

Sunk

MOTHER NATURE HAD WHIPPED-UP A DOOZY OF A COLD-weather recipe. At ten below, before factoring the winds sweeping off Long Lake, it was one of those January nights when the arctic air is quick to punish extremities and dig into the bones. Some might call it warden weather because nobody else is foolhardy enough to be outside. Fortunately, common sense was prevailing. Dennis McIntosh, along with fellow wardens Chris Cloutier, Neal Wykes, and Tim Place, were stationed on a snowmobile trail leading to the Long Lake end of the Naples Causeway. They were patrolling for snowmobilers who might have dipped too deep into the well at Rick's Cafe, a popular local watering hole. It was closing in on midnight and they hadn't seen a sled for several hours, which was a rarity for Saturday night.

"What do you think?" Dennis yelled to Neal from several feet away.

Neal held his hands up as if to say, "What?"

It was no wonder Neal couldn't hear him. The wind was howling through the trees and both men were wearing helmets with balaclavas underneath, a necessary layer in frostbite defense. Altogether, Dennis might as well have been dressed for a moon landing. Inside his black leather boots, he was wearing sock liners with thick wool socks. Long johns served as a base layer, over which he wore his warden uniform, followed by a bulky, full-body snowmobile suit. His thick, brown leather mittens were wool lined, in which Dennis massaged hand-warmer packets through his fingers. All of this clothing still wasn't enough to be standing around for hours on end. To compensate, the wardens paced the trail and did a variety of calisthenics to keep their body temperature up.

Dennis flipped his helmet's face shield up and stepped closer to Neal.

"There's not much point in staying out here any longer," he said, half yelling.

"I agree," Neal replied.

"What are you boys talking about?" Chris shouted as he joined the group.

"Leaving," Dennis told him.

"Already? But I'm on pace to break the Guinness record for jumping jacks."

"I don't want to see that," Neal said.

"Me either," Dennis agreed.

"Suit yourselves." Chris waved Tim over. "We're getting out of here."

"Ten-four," Tim said.

Dennis got on his snowmobile, a Ski-Doo he'd borrowed from Warden Christl Dorian. As a sergeant, Dennis no longer had the benefit of getting new equipment, often having to settle for hand-me-ups from the district wardens who reported to him. In this case, Christl's sled was brand new; however, it didn't come without a price.

"Be careful," she told him. "That's my baby. If there's so much as a scratch . . ."

"What do you think is going to happen?"

"You never know when wardens are involved. *Anything* can happen."

"Don't worry," Dennis said, "I'll take care of it."

"You better."

"It'll be good as new tomorrow."

"It is new!"

Dennis followed Chris's sled down the trail to Long Lake. While Neal and Tim had arrived from the Naples side, he and Chris had parked on the far end at the Harrison boat landing, so they had a ten-mile ride into the wind ahead of them. Once the trail spilled onto the vast, snow-covered lake, Dennis opened up the throttle and the sled eagerly met the challenge. In the blink of an eye, he was going fifty miles per hour and beginning to think better of it, Christl's threats still fresh in his mind. If he dumped the snowmobile over a snowdrift, she'd never let him hear the end of it, so he eased off the throttle and leveled the speed out at fifty. Consider it a compromise. Chris had no such qualms, and it wasn't long before he was a hundred yards ahead, his sled's red taillight a speck in the darkness.

There was something about flying across a lake at night, slicing through the stiff headwind without worry, the handlebar hand warmers working their magic; this was pure exhilaration. And to think Dennis was getting paid for this. Yeah, they weren't having a whole lot of fun for the majority of the evening, but it sure beat a desk job. A warden for twenty-five years, Dennis knew retirement wasn't far away, but he was in no hurry. He wouldn't trade his career for anything.

The snowmobile's headlight cast a swath of light before him, beyond which darkness stretched to the stars above. Dennis kept to the track laid by Chris as he scanned ahead for any snowdrifts. For the most part, it was smooth going, but then something looked strange. The headlights were shining off a large area of black ice that wasn't covered in snow. Dennis instantly knew what it was—a section of thin, newly formed ice.

Dennis squeezed the brakes and the snowmobile went into a full-on slide, the backside fishtailing to his right. He quickly realized his mistake, gunning the throttle in an attempt to regain speed. The sled swung back around as the track spun on the fresh ice. The snowmobile broke through and the back dropped into the water. Dennis kept his thumb pressed on the throttle. The engine screamed as the track churned water, slowly propelling the snowmobile forward. It wasn't doing much good, each inch of progress continued to break the ice, and there was still ten feet of black to go. The water came over Dennis's boots, then his knees. The sled was no longer moving forward. It was going under.

The front of the sled bobbed in the water as it sunk. Stepping onto the snowmobile seat, Dennis reached for the windshield to keep his balance. In the distance, Chris's taillight was shrinking. All of the black ice in front of Dennis had become open water, as was the case to his right. The ice sheet was intact on his left, but it was five or six feet away. He had no choice. Dennis leaped for the ice, his outstretched arms landing on the sheet, almost at his armpits, but there was too much force, and despite his desperate attempts to grip anything with his hands, his entire body slipped into the lake.

Dennis gasped as the frigid water seeped into his clothes and shocked his body, causing him to hyperventilate—fast, deep, chest-heaving breaths. His head had stayed above the surface, but the water pressing into his helmet went over his mouth and he sucked it in. Now he was choking and he couldn't quell the panic. Dennis tugged at the helmet, but it didn't budge. The chin strap dug into his throat. Kicking as hard as he could to keep his head above water, Dennis pulled off his gloves and unbuckled the strap.

He yanked away the helmet and pulled the balaclava opening off his mouth and under his chin, gasping for air.

Slowly, his breathing calmed.

He looked to the north.

Chris was gone.

Doing all he could to tread water, Dennis scanned the area, trying to get his bearings. Now that he was no longer staring into the light cast from the snowmobile, his eyes were adjusting and he saw shore. He was forty yards away, and judging from the black ice, at an inlet. That would explain his predicament. The inflowing water kept the lake from freezing at this spot until the most recent temperature plunge. It probably didn't help that Chris had passed over the ice first, likely weakening it, but Dennis's fate was sealed the moment he hit the brakes.

As a member of the Warden Service's search and rescue dive team, Dennis knew all too well the direness of his situation. Training had taught him that a person can survive for ten to twenty minutes in sub-forty-degree water, but the inevitability of hypothermia would draw blood to his core, causing his arms and legs to go weak. Already he could feel the effects sinking in. He'd expelled a lot of energy treading water while trying to get the helmet off, and his boots, multiple layers of clothes, and bulky snowmobile suit weren't doing him any favors. Nor was his build. His six-foot, 220-pound frame was an asset in most warden duties, but now it was working against him. All of which meant he was on the shorter end of the ten-to-twenty-minute scale.

Dennis worked his way to the edge of the ice and tried pulling himself up. His body refused. It had only been a couple of minutes, but his arms and legs were already depleted. There was no way he'd get out of the water unassisted.

How much longer could he tread water?

He was five or six miles from the Harrison boat landing. There simply wasn't time for Chris to get to the landing and come back.

And yet, Dennis kept looking north.

His only hope was that Chris would turn around before getting to the end of the lake. Maybe he'd check to make sure Dennis made it over the black ice?

Dennis didn't want to die.

He began yelling for help. Over and over again. It was borderline irrational and there was no way Chris could hear him, but maybe there was a camp nearby? He didn't know the lake all that well, even though they'd spent most of the day checking ice fishermen. Had they come near here?

Dennis continued to yell for what felt like an eternity.

Until he couldn't.

He gasped for breath, his arms and legs now heavier than he ever could have imagined. Each stroke felt as if he was being restrained. His mouth was slipping underwater and he was powerless to prevent it.

There was no way out.

No hope of rescue.

It was time to accept his fate.

This was the end.

"Lord," Dennis said aloud, spitting water from his mouth. "Please watch over my wife and daughters. Please give them strength."

And then he sank.

His head began to go under and his feet landed on something. Was this real or imagined? He picked up his right foot and set it down again. It was real! He was standing on the bottom of the lake, the water level just below his lips. It was a miracle, but he was far from safe. Water draws heat away from the body faster than air, and he was already on the cusp of losing control of his arms and legs. He had to get out.

The excitement of touching bottom gave him a shot of adrenaline, and he regained a slight measure of strength. Dennis edged his way to the solid ice. He held his breath and crouched until the water was at his nose. Then he leaped with all his might. His hands shot over the ice and he landed on the sheet at his elbows. He clawed at the ice and kicked the water behind him, but it wasn't enough; he was helpless as his body slipped back into the lake.

Dennis tried again, and once again he failed to stick to the ice. He looked up. Was that a light? Or was he seeing stars? No, it was coming from the north, and it was getting bigger.

Was it Chris coming back?

If Dennis could get out of the water, he just might live. He took a deep breath and closed his eyes, crouching until the water was prickling his forehead. Dennis leaped for the ice and landed at his armpits. This time, he stuck. He laid his head on the ice and caught his breath. From his training, Dennis knew to roll along the perimeter of the hole to get out of the water. The first flip brought him onto his back at his shoulders. The second flip to his chest. It was working—thank God, it was working! By the fourth his waist was out, and another two turns brought him far enough onto the ice that he could safely pull his feet up.

He tried to stand but his legs gave way. It was a bad idea, anyway. Dennis settled for getting to his knees and curling into a ball, keeping as much of his body from being exposed to the wind as he could. The next thing he knew, the rumble of Chris's snowmobile was beside him and he smelled exhaust.

"What are you trying to do?" Chris asked. "Where's your sled?"

"In the lake," Dennis said, pointing to the open water.

"Oh." Chris jumped off his sled and helped Dennis to his feet. "We've got to get you out of here."

Sitting on the back of the snowmobile, Dennis leaned into Chris to use him as a shield from the wind. Dennis was in shock and feeling no pain, but he was shaking uncontrollably. He wrapped his arms around Chris to keep his balance. Everything around him was a blur as they raced across the lake. He closed his eyes, wishing for the ride to be over. When they arrived at the boat landing, his arms and legs were covered in a layer of ice. He was literally frozen stiff.

The ice crackled as Dennis got to his feet and stumbled to his truck. Chris was calling to him, but Dennis had one thing in mind. He opened the driver's door and climbed in. After a moment of fumbling for his keys, he pulled them from his pocket and started the truck. The initial blast of cold air out of the vents did nothing to ease his shaking.

Chris opened the passenger door and climbed in.

"Christl's going to kill me," Dennis said, trying to act normal.

"I think you've got bigger problems right now," Chris said. "Look, buddy, we need to get you to a hospital."

"I'm fine."

"Dennis, this is serious. You need to get treated for hypothermia."

"I've got my faculties. I didn't get to the point of disorientation. Once this heater gets going, things will reverse. I'm not to the point of needing an IV, all they'll probably do in the hospital is wrap me in a heating blanket. I can do that at home."

Chris furrowed his brow. "Are you sure?"

"Yeah. The heat is kicking in. I'll be good to go in about ten."

"Alright, fine." Chris sighed. "I'm going to load the sled now and get my truck started. Don't go anywhere, let's see how you're doing when I'm done."

The heat was cranking now, which, with all the water in Dennis's clothes, turned the truck cab into a sauna. The windows filled with condensation and the defroster offered little relief. Dennis sat there shaking, unable to stop his teeth from chattering.

A rap on the window signaled Chris's return. "Are you sure you won't go to the hospital?"

"I'm good, thanks."

"Are you sure?"

"Yes."

"Okay. If you have any trouble, pull over and call me on the radio."

"I will."

Dennis wiped an area of the windshield clear with his hand and drove onto Route 117 toward Bridgton. It wasn't a hundred yards before he needed to wipe again, a pattern that continued for the entire hour-long drive home. Chris called several times to check on him, and by the time Dennis got home and stumbled through the front door, it was after 1:30 a.m. He discarded all of his clothing and yelled to his wife.

"Quiet," she said, coming down the stairs. Then she saw him. "Dennis—what in heaven's name—are you okay?"

"I went for a swim," he told her. "Carmen, I'm fine, I just need to warm up."

"You're shaking. Go get in the shower, I'll clean up the clothes."

Dennis headed for the stairs. Behind him, he heard Carmen mutter, "As if I didn't worry enough."

It was the longest, hottest shower of his life, and while it probably helped bring up his body temperature, the shaking persisted. Carmen was waiting for him when he got out with socks and a dry set of long johns. She'd also packed the bed with extra blankets. Dennis climbed under the covers and curled into a ball, a position he held for most of the night, the constant shivering fending off any possibility of sleep.

By morning, the shaking finally subsided, so Dennis did as game wardens do.

He went to work.

The first order of the day was getting Christl's snowmobile out of the lake. Relieved that Dennis was alive, she didn't give him any guff, which was saying something, because it couldn't have been fun riding around on a frozen seat for the next two months.

Chapter Twelve

The Game Farm Poachers

CHARLIE WAS DEAD. HIS BODY RESTED AGAINST THE DEER PEN'S chain-link fence, an arrow stuck behind his left front shoulder. Charlie was an impressive buck, even with a slightly ragged coat from continuously rubbing against the fence. Massive in stature and sporting a twelve-point rack, Charlie was easily one of the State Game Farm's feature attractions. At least, he had been.

"You didn't see or hear anything?" Warden Nat Berry asked Dave Wilbur, the Game Farm caretaker who lived on the premises.

"Not a peep," Dave said. "I'm typically a light sleeper, and I'm pretty sure I would have woken if they'd driven in here. My guess is they parked out by the road and walked in."

Nat agreed. He knew Dave well, so well, in fact, he thought it was a prank when he got the call earlier that morning. The Warden Service's regional headquarters in Gray was a mere half-mile from the Game Farm. Considering they were both agencies of the Maine Department of Inland Fisheries and Wildlife, it was unfathomable to think anyone would have the audacity to commit such a crime.

Dave unlocked the gate and they both entered the deer pen. Nat knelt next to Charlie to inspect the wound. It was a perfect shot, and by the looks of it, the only one needed to bring the buck down. That's not to say it had been difficult. There were pellets from the adjacent feed machine scattered around the pen.

"They used the feed to lure the deer up close," Nat said.

Dave sighed. "Yup. Wouldn't have been hard, the deer come to the fence at the mere sound of a dime getting turned into the machine. I wouldn't be surprised if they were able to rest the bow against Charlie."

"With their pick of the herd, they took the biggest one. How much does Charlie weigh?"

"Easily a hundred and eighty, if not more."

There were marks on the ground where Charlie had been dragged back to the fence, and multiple sets of footprints overlapping it all. Nat followed the scrape trail about thirty yards into the pen to where it ended.

"Charlie didn't make it very far," he said. "All the same, I don't think these guys did it for kicks. Why drag the deer back to the fence if you aren't trying to get it out?"

"To take a picture?" Dave suggested.

"I don't think so. They could have done that back here. They used a bow to avoid detection, why risk someone seeing a camera flash?"

Nat walked back to the fence, where, upon closer inspection, he noticed coarse, brown and gray hairs stuck in the chain links. Some of it was probably from deer rubbing against the fence, but several clumps were too high up to have gotten there without assistance.

"How high is this fence?" Nat asked.

"Eight feet. It has to be; any shorter and the deer can jump out. It also extends a couple feet into the ground so that nothing can dig in or out."

Nat shook his head. "Idiots. Had they gone after one of the smaller deer they might have been able to get it over, but Charlie, forget it. The worst part is they are probably going to get away with this. I hate to say it, but other than this arrow, we really don't have anything to go on." Nat knelt next to Charlie and pulled out the arrow. "Do you want me to dispose of Charlie for you?"

"Nah," Dave scoffed. "He's mountain lion meat now. I could use a hand getting him inside, though." Nat helped Dave drag Charlie into the barn, where Dave got to work gutting the deer and hanging him to bleed.

When Nat left, he was surprised to see a white van parked next to his department truck. After all, it was late November and the Game Farm was closed for the season. As he got closer, Nat recognized the call letters for the local CBS television affiliate, WGME, printed on the side of the van. Ross Hammons, a reporter Nat knew, got out and greeted him.

"Hello, Nate," Ross said, extending his hand. "Good to see you again."

Nat smiled and shook his hand. "Same here, but it's Nat."

"Oh, of course, I'm terribly sorry. I feel like I've made that mistake before."

"Don't worry about it, I get it a lot."

Ross adjusted his glasses. "Still, I'm sorry. I also hope you don't mind us showing up here, but we heard about the deer being killed over the scanner, and I talked to Chauncey Morris at the station and he told me we could find you here. Would you mind answering a few questions on camera?"

"Not at all," Nat said. He put on his red service coat and circular brim hat for the interview, which Ross wanted to shoot by the deer pen.

"Can you tell us what happened?" Ross asked, holding the microphone before Nat.

"Several suspects broke into the Game Farm late last night. They shot and killed a deer named Charlie at close range with a bow and arrow."

"What can you tell us about the suspects?"

"Judging by the footprints, they are believed to be male. We don't know exactly how many people were involved, but there were at least two."

"Can you speculate on a motive?"

"It's difficult to say why someone would do this, other than they probably saw the deer as an easy target." Nat paused for a second, choosing his words carefully. "Hunting is supposed to be a sport, but there wasn't anything sporting about this. The deer here are social animals that trust people. It's an unfortunate incident that we are taking very seriously."

"That's great, thanks. I think we got what we need."

"No problem." Nat shook Ross's hand and began to walk back to his vehicle, only to stop. "Look, Ross, off the record, we really don't have much to go on here. I know you don't divulge your sources, but we could use some help."

"Say no more. We'll ask for anyone with information to contact the Warden Service or to call the television station directly. It's not a problem if they know upfront how the information is going to be used."

"Thanks. I really appreciate it."

The story ran as the lead on the six o'clock news that night and over the next few days the phones rang off the hook. Several people called to describe vehicles they had seen in the Gray area carrying dead deer in the middle of the day. One older gentleman didn't actually see a deer in the vehicle, but claimed, "You know, it looked like that kind of truck." There was also a woman who specifically wanted to know if the deer killed was her son's favorite.

And of course, there was the chorus of people demanding that the poachers be brought to justice.

"It never ceases to amaze me," Lieutenant Chauncey Morris said to Nat while they were reviewing the leads, or lack thereof. "People turn a blind eye to poaching every day, but the second they see it on TV, everyone is all up in arms."

"Everyone loves Bambi," Nat said.

Later that day they finally got a break. Ross called with the name and number of a woman who reached out. Nat immediately got her on the phone to ask why she contacted the television station.

"Well," the woman started to say in a soft, timid voice as if she was embarrassed by what she had to say. "I was at a bar in the Old Port last night and I, um, met this guy. He was really drunk and bragging about breaking into the Game Farm."

"Do you know his name?"

"Not his real name, but everyone was calling him Moose."

"Moose?"

"Yeah. He was a real big guy. Not fat. Just big. But he did have a gut."

"What else did he look like?"

"It's hard to say. I was drinking and it was dark and everything in the bar. All I remember is that he had scraggly brown hair and a baby face."

"So you don't actually know him?"

"No. I'm sorry, I'm not much help."

"It's okay. What about anyone you were with, did they know him? Or did you know anyone he was with?"

"I'm sorry, no. Meeting him was totally random. He was with a couple of guys, they were all pretty drunk, and they just started talking to us. To be honest, they kinda sketched us out and we got away from them as soon as we could. I'm really sorry if I'm not much help."

"It's okay, really, you can stop apologizing. Is there anything else that you remember, anything at all?"

"Not that I can think of . . . well, actually, I don't know if this will help or not, but he was hurt. He had crutches. Something or other with his knee. Said he did it climbing over the fence."

"Really? That may be helpful information." Nat asked a few more questions before thanking the woman for her time. He hung up and yelled down the hall to Chauncey, "We got something!"

Lieutenant Morris was relatively new to his supervisory role. Like many wardens moving up through the ranks, he was slow to relinquish fieldwork and embrace the administrative aspect of his new position. It was no surprise to Nat that Chauncey was more than happy to get out from behind his desk and help follow the lead to the local hospitals. Their first stop was Maine Medical Center in Portland.

"I'm sorry," the woman at the front desk said. "I can't give out patient information."

"We understand," Nat said. "All we're asking is for you to tell us whether a man with a leg injury came in on Tuesday night. You don't have to give us a name or any other identifiable information."

"I'm sorry, I can't, it's hospital policy."

"You realize this is information we can legally obtain with a court subpoena," Chauncey said. "We're trying to determine whether this is necessary, and a simple yes or no can save everyone a lot of headaches."

The woman pursed her already thin lips at Chauncey. "You'll have to get your subpoena. I can't help you."

They returned to the truck empty handed.

"That went well," Nat said. "I was thinking about it, and I know we're checking the Portland hospitals because the woman I talked to met Moose in Portland, but he could have gone to Lewiston."

"It's possible," Chauncey agreed. "Lewiston would have been closer."

"If we keep getting stonewalled, are we going to get subpoenas for all the hospitals in the region?"

"We might have to."

The next stop was Mercy Hospital in Portland. At the front desk they were directed to the head nurse, a short, enthusiastic woman named Janice.

"Is this about the Game Farm incident?" she wanted to know. "My daughter loves it there. I try to take her a couple of times each summer. She likes the deer, but the mountain lions are her favorite. I always have to bribe her with candy just to move on."

"My daughters love it there, too," Nat said. "We have reason to believe that one of the men who broke in injured his leg, possibly his knee. Do you know if anyone fitting this description was admitted Tuesday night?"

"I do. I was on duty that night, and yes, there was."

Nat and Chauncey exchanged looks.

"He tore his right MCL," Janice went on to say. "I remember him in particular because he refused pain medication. Very adamant about it, too. I got the feeling he'd had a substance problem." Janice grabbed a clipboard from the nurse's station and flipped back a couple of pages. "Please understand that I can't disclose any personal information."

"We know," Chauncey said. "You've already been very helpful."

Janice smiled. She placed the clipboard on the counter and turned it to face Nat and Chauncey. Her index finger was fixed on a name: Stewart Cooper.

"Have a good day, gentlemen," she said. "And good luck with the investigation." With that she walked away, having left the clipboard in front of them. Adjacent to Moose's real name was his address and telephone number.

"What do you say we pay Moose a visit?" Chauncey said.

— ⁓ —

The address brought them to a three-story apartment building on Munjoy Hill. The place looked to be a gust of wind away from being condemned. The exterior paint, originally white, turned overcast with age, was visibly peeling. The banister that accompanied the front steps was on the lawn.

"Looks like we're going to the third floor," Nat said. He pointed to the black mailbox adjacent to the front door with the number three on it. There was a small strip of paper taped to the box, where the name "Cooper" was displayed.

They entered the building to find two unchained Dobermans guarding the first-floor apartment. The dogs showed their teeth and growled in unison, but otherwise made no attempt to get up. There was just enough room for Nat and Chauncey to skirt around them. Nat went up the stairs first. His heavy boots created a hollow thud with each step and the wooden boards creaked beneath his weight.

"We might as well have called ahead," Nat said.

"Not a bad idea," Chauncey said. "Maybe they could have prepared lunch."

There was no welcome mat or any other decorations outside the third-floor apartment. An outline of the number three appeared on the stained wooden door in a lighter shade, presumably where the apartment number had once hung. Nat knocked. There was some commotion inside and it sounded like someone yelled, "Just a minute." True to the promise, a woman answered the door about a minute later. It was midday and yet her hair was up in curlers and she was wearing a pink bathrobe. She looked to be forty-five going on fifty-five.

"How did you get past the dogs?" the woman asked. She was holding a lit cigarette inches from her mouth.

"We're game wardens," Chauncey said. "That's how."

She seemed to accept this at face value. "What do you want?"

"We're looking for Moose," Nat said, watching the woman's reaction to see if she recognized the name. "Is he home?"

The woman turned inside. "Moose," she yelled, "some wardens here for you."

"Bring 'em in," a man shot back. "You know I can't get up."

She gestured with a wave of her head for them to enter. The front door accessed the kitchen, which, in addition to cigarette smoke, also smelled of nail polish. A green, fold-up card table was positioned in the center of the room, where the woman sat down and resumed doing her nails. She took a drag off her cigarette before saying with a nod to the living room, "He's in there."

Moose was sitting on a couch with his right leg propped on a coffee table and an Atari joystick in his hand. He fit the description: big and baby-faced. It was safe to say Moose hadn't shaved in a week, and yet the accumulated growth amounted to nothing more than sparse whiskers. The hair on top of his head looked as flustered as he was.

"Are you Moose?" Nat asked.

The man nodded.

"Is your real name Stewart Cooper?"

"Yeah," Moose said. "What's this about?"

In the background, the television made an unfortunate sound. Nat glanced over to see Pac-Man caught by the ghosts.

"Look, Moose," Nat said. "We know you were involved with the deer killed at the Game Farm. What we don't know is who was with you. The best thing for you to do is to come clean and tell us everything; otherwise, you're going to take the fall for this and the punishment will be worse."

Moose put the joystick down. "I'll tell you anything you want to know. Shit, it wasn't my idea. I didn't wanna go in the first place."

"Why did you?" Chauncey asked.

"I don't know. One minute we were drinking and playing cards, and the next thing I knew we were out of booze and John was talking about killing a deer at the Game Farm. He said it would be easy, and that he'd take the deer to get tagged in the morning. John's in one of those big buck contests with a couple thousand dollars on the line. He said he'd split the pot with us. Randy was all in, so what was I supposed to do? I didn't want to be the pussy."

"But you did end up getting hurt," Nat said.

"Yeah. I screwed up my knee pretty good. My jeans got caught on the fence when I was climbing over and I fell into the pen. Not to brag, but I was the muscle, so once I got hurt, those guys stood no chance of getting the deer out. It was all we could do just to get me out."

"Who shot the deer?" Nat asked.

"John. It was his bow. I've never even been hunting before."

"This isn't the way to start."

"Yeah. Figured as much. So what happens now? Am I going to jail?"

"Not today. I'm going to issue you a summons for night hunting and for killing a deer at the Game Farm. It's all up to the judge, of course, but you'll probably only get a fine, especially since you've cooperated."

Moose continued to play along, disclosing John and Randy's full names and whereabouts. Randy was an easy find; however, he wasn't as cooperative as Moose. Not that it mattered. With Moose's testimony as evidence, Randy eventually confessed. It was John who proved to be a problem. His official residence was in Portland, but he was nowhere to be found. Most likely Moose or Randy had tipped him off. Nat and Chauncey were able to track him to a house in Bethel, but that turned up empty, too. They were beginning to think John didn't exist when Nat got another helpful telephone call, this time from Alex Grover, an attorney from Lewiston.

"I'm representing John Magee," Alex said. "He knows that you're looking for him and he's afraid he'll get sent to Thomaston."

Nat laughed. He couldn't help it. "That's ridiculous. He'll most likely get a five-hundred-dollar fine and maybe a few days in jail. He's definitely not going to prison."

"Trust me, I know, but there's no talking any sense to him."

"Even if I talk to him myself?"

"He definitely doesn't want that. For whatever reason, he's scared to death of you guys."

"This is crazy. I have to issue him a summons."

"I know. That's why I'm calling. Would it be possible for you to send the summons to me? I'll make sure my client gets it."

Nat paused for a moment. "I suppose that'll work."

❧

A week later Nat went into the dry cleaners in Gray to pick up his uniforms. Elaine, a cheerful woman who was fond of ribbing him, greeted Nat at the counter.

"Boy, Nat," she said. "You're awful tough on the people you pinch for poaching." Elaine continued to talk over her shoulder as she turned to retrieve his uniforms from the oval rack. "I hope you're never after me for anything."

"What do you mean?"

"Here we go." She plopped a week's worth of uniforms onto the counter. "You know, that guy who killed the deer at the Game Farm."

"What about him?"

Elaine dropped her smile. "You really don't know?"

"Know what?"

"Just a minute." She turned around again, this time, to grab a newspaper. "Here, read for yourself."

Elaine had handed him the newspaper. Nat scanned the page and immediately saw what she was referencing: *PORTLAND— John Magee, 29, of Portland was found dead in his apartment late Tuesday evening, an apparent suicide.* Nat skimmed forward. *Magee was recently charged with killing a deer at the State Game Farm in Gray.*

When he returned to the station, Nat bypassed the receptionist and went straight to his office. He called Alex Grover.

"Don't beat yourself up over this," Alex said. "John had more problems in his life than you could have known. In the last couple of months, his wife left him and he subsequently lost his job. Suffice it to say, he was a bulb that wasn't screwed in straight, and as the saying goes, the deer was just the straw on the camel's back."

"I can't help but think . . ."

"Well, don't. You were only doing your job."

Nat thanked Alex for his time and hung up the phone. He gripped the arms of his chair as if he was going to get up, but instead leaned back and stared out the window. He wasn't looking at anything in particular. Then the phone rang. It was dispatch, a hiker was missing in Grafton Notch.

CHAPTER THIRTEEN

A Catch for Satan

"REMIND ME," WARDEN JOHN FORD SAID. "WHY'D YOU VOLUN-
teer us for this?"

"Don't start," Warden Bill Allen said in a raspy growl. He and
John often worked together, and they were good friends, so he
knew he was being goaded. Bill tried to dismiss John by looking
through the green filter of his night-vision scope for the umpteenth
time that evening. He eyed a small cape house with weathered gray
shingles for siding and an attached shed in back. It looked like
most any Down East home, but it wasn't just another house to Bill.

"What? It's a fair question. I'm curious what stroke of good
fortune has us here at two in the morning, for the second night
in a row, watching a house in which the occupants have the good
sense to be sleeping."

"You know why," Bill said.

They'd landed this assignment after Bill, fresh out of a certifi-
cation course on identifying potential drug operations, learned that
his in-laws had sold their house to a couple from Florida for cash.
The transaction was suspicious, but he couldn't help thinking that
perhaps the course had him a little overzealous. Even so, it was still
a house, paid for in cash. Who, with that kind of money, wants to
move from Florida to Stockton Springs, Maine?

So Bill started driving by the house whenever he was in the neighborhood, which did nothing to alleviate his suspicions. In addition to the occupants, several RV campers and a greenhouse had moved onto the lot. One would think multiple campers and a greenhouse would mean lots of outside activity, but he rarely saw a soul. When an actual person was spotted, it was often a male, mid-twenties, going to or from a station wagon. Forget about buying the house with cash in hand, what kid with that kind of money drives a station wagon?

Confident he had enough to go on, Bill contacted the State Police. They confirmed his suspicions. In fact, they'd known about the house for some time, and, since Bill was now in the know and he had intimate knowledge of the property, they could sure use his and the Warden Service's help. The house was part of a much larger operation run by the Florida-based Zion Coptic Church. A ship out of Columbia was hauling marijuana to Stonington, where the drugs would be unloaded and transported to the Stockton Springs house for processing and packaging into movable units. Once street-ready, the marijuana would be loaded into the RVs and shipped as far away as California. Thanks to an inside informant, the federal Drug Enforcement Administration and the Maine State Police knew the boat was coming; they just didn't know when it would arrive. It was Bill and John's job to watch the house for any irregular behavior that might indicate an imminent arrival.

"Look," Bill said, "they're drug dealers . . . it was something different . . . I thought it'd be fun."

"Yep, a real pisser," John said.

Bill sighed. "I know."

"It doesn't take a warden to figure out why the Staties pegged us for house duty."

"I know." Bill wasn't taking the bait. Not this time.

That didn't stop John from trying. "Don't get me wrong, I appreciate you thinking of me for this wild adventure. Given the choice, though, I have to say I prefer working a field for poachers."

"There's a field behind us. Knock yourself out."

"Don't tease me."

They were stationed in Bill's cruiser, parked along a knoll that was half a football field from the house and hidden amongst a pine grove. The car's exterior and interior lights had been shut off a mile before arrival to avoid detection, and the back half of the car was covered with a parachute, making it nearly impossible to see them from the remote country road. Beyond the road was an expansive blueberry barren. It was a quiet, cloudless, gibbous moon evening with good visibility. Nary a car had passed since their arrival six hours earlier. The only sound to be heard was Bill's dog Satan, a German shepherd that he'd trained himself and was department sanctioned, snoring in the back seat.

"I gotta go," John said, holding up an empty coffee cup as evidence and quietly opening the passenger door.

"I didn't notice this before," John said upon returning. "There are ham radio antennae wires strung through the pine trees above us. This must be how the house maintains contact with the ship."

"If only we could hear what was being communicated," Bill said. He again trained his scope on the house. He couldn't escape the memories of nervously knocking on the front door to pick up his future wife on dates, which eventually led to Thanksgiving dinners and Christmas feasts with the family. Never in his wildest dreams did he imagine he'd be casing the place. "All this waiting around for signs of drug activity wouldn't be necessary."

"For what it's worth," John said, "I scanned the field while I was out. Nothing happening there, either."

Bill unrolled his window and took a deep breath of the crisp October air.

"I got one for you," John said. "Remember the Unity student that hung himself in the house on Quaker Hill?"

"Remember?" Bill said, excited. "I got the call with you on that one. When I got there, two Unity students were standing at the edge of the driveway. They'd come by to go bird hunting, and as they neared the house, they could smell something awful. They swore they hadn't gone in."

"Oh, I'd bet they did."

"No doubt. You could smell it from where they were. One of 'em said to me, "Go over there, you can look in from the corner window." It was the damnedest thing I ever saw. The guy hung himself on top of the refrigerator—how long had he been there?"

"A month."

"Right. He was still sitting there on the refrigerator, the noose holding him in place. It was beyond disturbing. His skin had turned just as black as could be. He looked like an orangutan."

"And all of his bright orange hair had fallen out. It looked like the fringe of a woman's coat around his sneakers, glowing a bit in the sunlight coming through the window."

The appearance of headlights on the road behind them stole their attention. Both wardens turned in their seats to watch the car pass, but it didn't appear suspicious.

"Probably someone coming home from the bar," Bill said.

"Right. As I was saying," John continued with his story. "A week or so later I was driving past the house with Dave Bailey, and Dave asks where the guy hung himself, so we go take a look. We poked around a bit and were about to leave when Dave says to me, 'Fordy, someone's looking out the upper window.' Dave's always screwing around so I didn't believe him. He says, 'No, I'm telling you someone's in the house.' I play along and go and knock on the door, thinking it's a joke.

"All of a sudden the door swings open and a guy is standing there that looks exactly like the kid who hung himself—same red hair, same build, same flannel shirt, same everything. My knees buckled and I couldn't say a word. Turns out the kid had a twin brother from Alaska that nobody knew about, but I sure as hell thought I'd seen a—"

The unmistakable boom of a shotgun echoed across the field. Satan jumped up and started barking.

"Quiet!" Bill commanded, and Satan immediately stopped barking. He anxiously moved from one side window to the other, his tail whacking the back seat.

"I'll get the parachute," John said.

Bill started the car and looked through his scope at the house, making sure the shot and their commotion didn't wake the residents. After giving it a couple minutes without any lights coming on, and waiting for John to get back in, he drove the car down to the road, turned around, and then backed it into the same spot so they were now facing the field. He killed the engine, and through the scope, he could see the suspects get out of a car further down the road.

"There are two men," Bill reported. "One is carrying the shotgun, the other looks to have a knife in his hand. They're working this way through the field."

"Okay," John said. "I'll run down the road and sneak in on the backside. When I turn my flashlight on, you light this field up like Fenway."

"Ten-four."

Through the green of the scope, Bill watched the poachers work their way across the field. It wasn't a commercial blueberry barren, so it was overgrown and slow going for the men. Along the road, he could see John ducking down and bobbing along the tree line. Scanning back to the poachers, a deer—a good-sized buck—sprung from its hiding spot. The deer was hobbling, apparently having been shot in one of the hind quarters. The men saw it, too. The guy in the lead, the one with the knife, pointed at the deer. This was getting dangerous, as the buck was headed directly for John, putting him in the line of fire. John moved behind a large pine. The men started high-stepping through the bushes, trying to catch the deer. As the buck reached the end of the field and crossed the road, the man with the shotgun raised to fire. Bill turned to the deer. It scampered into the woods and ran right past John.

Expecting a gunshot that didn't occur, Bill once again spied the men. The one with the knife reached the road first and there was a sudden flash of light that blinded Bill's view. He put down the scope and turned on the car's headlights. John was on the road with his flashlight and pistol fixed on the man with the knife. The guy turned his head back to the field, appearing to yell at his buddy, before tossing the knife aside and getting down on his knees. John laid him on the road and handcuffed his hands behind his back. Bill got out of the car and looked into the field. The second poacher was nowhere to be seen.

"Where'd the other guy go?" Bill yelled to John.

John raised his hands as if to say he didn't know. "Send in the dog!"

"You hear that?" Bill called to the missing man. "The dog is coming in. If I were you, I'd give up."

Nothing.

"Bad choice!" Bill yelled. He opened the car's back door and grabbed Satan by the collar. The dog pulled him back across the road. "He thinks we're bluffing," Bill said to himself before yelling, "Get 'em, Satan!"

Satan shot into the field like a missile, picking up on the man's scent within seconds. The bushes parted in a nearly straight line where Satan raced through.

"I give up!" the man shouted, getting to his knees. Looking directly at Satan barreling toward him, he raised his hands in the air. "I give up! I give up!"

"Noooo!" Bill yelled.

It was too late.

Satan tried to stop but couldn't hold up. The massive dog skidded into the man and bunted him in the face, sending him sprawling backward. Bill ran into the field and moments later he found the man lying face-down in the bushes, covering his head with his arms. Satan stood over him, growling. The man was trembling as Bill helped him to his feet.

"H-how l-long have you guys had them f-fuckin' dogs?" the man stammered.

Bill was tempted to tell the man he was lucky to have only run into Satan. Hunting near this house was surely tempting fate. Not wanting to blow their cover, he bit his tongue.

Given the circumstances for why they were there, the wardens issued summons to the men instead of arresting them on the spot. It was the first time Bill and John had ever done so. Once all the paperwork was taken care of and the men had driven away, Bill turned to John and asked if he was ready to go back to watching the house.

John smiled. "Seems like the least we could do."

Chapter Fourteen

To Catch 'Em, Join 'Em

When Anita Harris donated the 1,230 acres of land for the Holbrook Island Sanctuary in Brooksville to the State of Maine in 1971, the sanctuary came with protection. Harris had hired a former Connecticut State Police officer to guard the land and its natural resources. One of Harris's conditions of the gift was that the officer keep the job until he retired, which he did in the fall of 1975. No love was lost at this news by locals who lived on the shady side of gaming laws, and when the Department of Conservation hadn't found a suitable replacement at the time of retirement, the sanctuary essentially became an all-you-can-poach buffet for several weeks.

Coastal Warden Jim Brown drove into the sanctuary and backed his car into the woods. Since the sanctuary had been under private security, this was the first time he or anyone else had gone in on warden business. Jim pulled the camouflage parachute over his white Plymouth Fury and set off on foot for the orchard at the beginning of the Indian Bar Road. It was a crisp October night and the crackling sound of his boots gripping the dirt road pierced the evening quiet. The taste of ocean was in the air, and the moonlight was bright enough for him to see without a flashlight.

As soon as Jim reached the intersection, lights appeared from a car approaching in the opposite direction on the Back Road. The car would have seemed odd to most people as it looked to have three headlights, but Jim had no doubt as to why there was a third light. He scampered into the orchard on the inside turn of the intersection and lay under an apple tree. The car slowed to make the turn. It looked to be a dark-colored Pontiac with four doors. A person in the front passenger seat was holding a spotlight over the top of the vehicle to light the orchard. The back-seat window on the driver's side was open, and a rifle barrel protruded from the window frame.

Jim regretted his choice of a hiding spot. As a coastal warden for the Department of Sea and Shore Fisheries, he wore a uniform that consisted of a tan shirt and dark-brown pants. Lying in the wet grass, he could easily be mistaken for a bedded deer. Jim lowered his head, closed his eyes, and held his breath as the car drove by and the spotlight passed over him. No shots rang out and the vehicle continued along without any noticeable change.

"Close one," Jim whispered to himself.

The Indian Bar Road was a dead end, so the vehicle had to come back. There wasn't time to get his car, nor did Jim want to stay put—one game of spotlight chicken was enough for the night. He could stand in the road and flag the car down, but then they'd unload the gun and he'd only be able to nab them for spotlighting. And that's assuming they stopped. Whatever he was going to do, he had to make it quick, because the car's headlights were already breaking around a bend in the road. Jim ran across the intersection and ducked behind a maple tree. On the car's return trip, the spotlight was again aimed into the orchard, which meant the shooter likely switched seats in the back. Jim's suspicion was confirmed when the car slowed to make the right turn in front of him and there was no gun pointing in his direction.

Without waiting for rational thought to corral his impulse, Jim charged the car. He got a hold of the handle on the back door and jumped into the empty seat.

If synchronized swearing were an Olympic sport, the three men in the car nailed gold. The driver slammed on the brakes and everyone braced themselves. Now they were the ones looking like deer in headlights.

"Warden," Jim said in his best attempt at a conversational tone, trying to diffuse the situation. "What are you boys up to tonight?"

CHAPTER FIFTEEN

Spider Lake Rescue

"JACK, YOU'VE OUTDONE YOURSELF," WARDEN PILOT GARY DUMOND said, admiring the plate of fried chicken, mashed potatoes and gravy, and steamed carrots coated with a river of butter that fellow warden pilot Jack McPhee placed before him.

"Careful," Jack replied, "you shouldn't compliment the cook until you've taken a bite."

"You haven't killed me yet."

"Well, there's a first time for everything."

It was February of 1973, and Gary had spent the day flying Ted Cyr, the department's photographer, around the various ponds and lakes of northwestern Maine. Ted was doing a feature on Ray Porter, also known as the "Flying Beaver Trapper." Ray was an older pilot Gary had known since he was a kid who owned an air service out of Shin Pond. In the winter, Ray closed down the business and turned his focus to trapping. By outfitting one of his Piper Super Cubs with skis, he was able to reach ponds that other trappers couldn't, and he covered far more area in a day than anyone else. The number of pelts Ray would get in a season was already the envy of the trapping community.

After a fun day of tailing Ray, Gary and Ted were taking the opportunity to catch up with Jack for a night at his camp on Spider Lake.

"Can you believe Ray has caught almost four hundred beaver this year?" Ted said.

Before anyone could answer, a knocking sound interrupted their conversation.

"Did you hear that?" Jack asked.

"I think someone's at the door," Gary said.

"Can't be," Jack scoffed. "The road isn't plowed, and there's only one other active camp on the lake; it's a seasonal rental for ice fisherman. I don't need to tell you how often the clientele seeks out their friendly neighborhood warden."

There was another knock at the door.

"Didn't you just say there's a first time for everything?" Gary said. Jack started to slide his chair back, but Gary beat him to the punch.

At the door was a man dressed in a full-body snowmobile suit, thick gloves, a blue winter hat with a yellow pompom, and ski goggles resting on his forehead. His face was a lively red from sledding on the lake, but he also wore a look of urgency that's all too familiar to wardens.

"Please," the man said. "We've had an accident. My buddy's hurt—it's bad."

"Where is he?"

"Across the lake at the ledges. He must not have seen them, hit 'em full throttle."

"We'll get our stuff."

Gary and Jack quickly pulled on their boots and wool wardens' coats.

"Can I come?" Ted asked.

"Yes," Jack said. "Bring your camera."

"Let's take my plane," Gary said as they followed the snow-mobiler out the door. "It's probably still warm." A ten-degree chill greeted them outside along with a moderate snowfall that had collected about two inches on the plane in the hour since they arrived. Gary and Jack removed the wing covers and dusted off the windshield. The two wardens and Ted climbed into the Cessna 185 Skywagon, a six-seater with the back two seats removed for gear storage. Wheel-skis had been attached to the plane for winter, enabling them to taxi across the two feet of snow blanketing the frozen lake. Following the snowmobile's red taillight, it only took a couple of minutes to travel the mile to the ledges.

They'd entered a nightmare. The headlights from four idling snowmobiles illuminated two men lying unconscious in the snow. Neither had helmets on, and both looked severely injured. The worse of the two was bleeding from his nose, mouth, and even ears. He also had a laceration across his throat. Blood was everywhere, soaked into their clothes, and melting into the snow. The snowmobile they'd been riding, a black Arctic Cat, was overturned, the front smashed, frame bent, and a ski broken entirely off. Gary shined his light on the cliffs, which protruded out at a point. There were dark red streaks smeared onto the rock face, along with black marks from the snowmobile. The tracks leading up to the cliff showed they'd hit the point at a sharp angle—probably moving at a good forty miles per hour on impact. A flash of light from Ted's camera drew Gary's attention to a nearly empty gallon bottle of Allen's Coffee Brandy lying among the strewn debris from the snowmobile's fiberglass hood, windshield, and headlight casing.

"Jack, you better go preflight your plane," Gary said. "Both of these guys have to get to a hospital ASAP."

"Take me back to the cabin," Jack said to the man who'd knocked on his door.

"No problem."

"I'm driving," Jack told him.

"Still no problem."

"I'll get this guy out of here," Gary said, pointing to the man with the throat laceration. "He's the most critical." As he said this, Gary knew it was splitting hairs with a God-like decision. Both men were in dire need of emergency care. The extra time it would take to get the second man onto Jack's plane could very well be the difference between life and death. Even so, Gary only had room for one.

There were three other men from the fishing party milling around the scene. Gary was about to address them when another snowmobile pulled up. The driver jumped off his sled and ran over carrying two sacks.

"I've got sleeping bags," the man said to Gary, huffing and puffing.

"Good thinking," Gary said. "Bring one of those with me." Gary led the man to his plane. "I'm going to take the co-pilot seat and the one behind it on the right out. Get the sleeping bag ready and we'll put it on the floor here for your buddy to lay on." Gary quickly removed the seats and went back for the injured man.

"You three," Gary said, pointing to the remaining fishermen. "Two of you get his legs, one of you at his shoulders on the other side of me." Gary squatted next to the injured man's left shoulder, and the others followed suit. He looked each of them in the eye. There was no question they'd all been drinking, but they were wired with adrenaline now. "We need to be extremely careful. It's very likely he has a spinal injury. I'll hold his head; we all need to lift in unison to keep him as straight and flat as possible—does everyone understand?"

They all answered yes.

"Good. Lift on three. One . . . two . . . THREE!"

The injured man's body rose as evenly as expected under the circumstances. The sudden movement caused him to gag, blood spilling from his mouth, creating wide-eyed reactions from the fishermen.

"Don't let up!" Gary barked. "Slow and careful to the passenger side."

Like pallbearers, they carried the man to the plane.

"Get in," Gary said to the fisherman who'd put down the sleeping bag. "We'll feed him to you."

Getting the man through the plane's single door and laid onto his back in the cramped space along the right side of the aircraft was a trick unto itself. It wasn't perfect to say the least, but none of them were EMS personnel, so they did the best they could, as quick as they could. They situated the injured man with his head at the front of the plane under the instrument panel. The sleeping-bag man stayed aboard to help, sitting in the lone seat behind Gary. In what seemed like no time at all, the engine was roaring and the propellers pulled them forward.

The plane sped down the lake. Due to the snow, Gary didn't bother turning on the takeoff lights. In the faint light from the instrument panel, he could tell the windows had become fogged from all the heavy breathing. The fogging was a new challenge Gary hadn't encountered before, but it didn't matter. In snowy conditions like this, he'd never try to land on a lake at night, and certainly not with fogged windows. But takeoff was a different story. His instruments and knowledge of the lake were all he needed to clear the tall pines lining the shore and the hill beyond. Once the plane exceeded fifty miles per hour, Gary pushed in the throttle, and the aircraft climbed steeply into the night. Looking down, he could faintly see the light of Jack's plane taxiing back across the lake. Gary turned on his lights so Jack could see that he'd taken off. A thick squall created a whiteout within the light that erased any view of Jack's plane.

Gary's plane climbed at a rate of a thousand feet per minute. Once it reached 3,500 feet, safely above any of the mountains on their flight path, Gary leveled the plane off for cruising and turned his attention to notifying emergency services. It's a thirty-minute flight from Spider Lake to Presque Isle, which he hoped would give them enough time to have assistance ready. He radioed the State Police barracks in Houlton and informed them of the situation; they'd need two ambulances at the Presque Isle airport for two flights approximately fifteen minutes apart.

Despite the winter storm, there wasn't any turbulence disrupting the flight. The cabin warmed up to a comfortable temperature and the windows cleared. The roar of the engine, however, made it difficult to talk to the passenger who'd come along to help, and yet the suffocating gurgling and gagging sounds the injured man was making were all too clear. The man's head was below Gary's right knee and slightly under the instrument panel, the faint light from which illuminated the blood, bruising, and bloating that made his face nearly unrecognizable as that of a person.

"He's choking," Gary yelled to the man's friend. "If you don't get his airways open, he's going to drown in his blood."

"What do I do?" the friend asked.

"Stick your fingers in his mouth, try to move his tongue and whatever else is blocking his throat out of the way. Get any blood out you can, just be careful of his neck."

The friend spooned out gobs of blood and what looked like a tooth with his fingers. Gary turned away and checked his watch for something to do. Ten past nine. Not even an hour earlier he'd been drooling over the plate of food Jack put before him, and now he didn't have the slightest appetite. It was a stroke of luck that the accident occurred on a lake where two warden pilots just happened to be staying for the night. Had it occurred on any of the other ponds or lakes in the area, or on any other night, there was no doubt these two men were about to become obituaries. While that still may be their fate, Gary retraced the night's events in his mind, and he knew they'd done everything they possibly could.

So why did he feel so helpless?

The sky cleared and all of a sudden they could see the stars above and the lights of Ashland below, followed by those of Presque Isle. Everything always looked closer at night.

The injured man was choking and gagging again.

They couldn't get there fast enough. Gary tuned the radio to Presque Isle airport's advisory channel and grabbed the microphone.

"PQI, this is a Warden Service Cessna 185 out of Spider Lake with a passenger in critical condition. We're ten miles out, approaching from the southwest."

"Cessna 185," air traffic control responded, "We're expecting your arrival. You're number one in the queue; the north-south runway is yours. Emergency services are waiting at the terminal."

Continuing to listen to the advisory channel, Gary learned that air traffic control was holding up two Northeast Airlines passenger flights for his arrival. He flicked on his landing lights, aligned the plane with the main runway, and began the descent. On the way down, Gary pumped the hydraulic lever that switched the landing gear from skis to wheels about thirty times to make the change. The plane came in without a hitch and no sooner did he taxi off the main runway than the first of the two Northeast Airlines flights landed.

The area outside the terminal was awash in flashing red light from two ambulances. Once the plane was parked and it was safe to exit, Gary and the injured man's friend got out of the way. The EMTs put a cervical collar on the injured man and maneuvered him out on a backboard. About the time the first ambulance pulled away, Jack's plane arrived.

Gary went back to his plane. It was a mess of dark puddles on the floor and blood soaked into the sleeping bag. He wasn't looking forward to the cleanup because he knew it would all freeze before he got the chance.

A hand appeared on Gary's shoulder. It was Jack.

"What do you say we grab a cup of coffee?"

"Yeah," Gary said. "I'm not quite ready for this."

They hitched a ride with a police officer to a nearby coffee shop and settled into a booth.

"Did you have any trouble on takeoff?" Jack asked.

"Not really," Gary said. "You?"

"I'd say so—nearly hit the island. I saw it at the last moment as the plane was lifting off, and I had to drag a wingtip in the snow to avoid it."

"Good evening, gentlemen," the waitress said, arriving with a pot of coffee. She poured each of them a cup. "I'll be back in a minute to see if I can fill your bellies with anything else."

Gary sat there for a moment, staring at his coffee. He'd completely forgotten that they hadn't eaten.

"I can't shake the sound of the guy choking on his blood," Gary said. "It was unlike anything I've ever heard before. Inhuman, almost. Can't imagine I'll ever forget it."

"Be glad it was only sounds that your guy was making," Jack said. "The guy I had came to at one point." He paused for a second of thought. "Well, 'came to' probably isn't the best way to describe it. The slits of his eyes opened as far as they could, and he sat up, but he was right out of it, clearly in shock. He started reaching and grabbing for anything he could. Nearly ripped the radio microphone out, and then he got ahold of the throttle. If it wasn't for his friend pinning him down, he just might have crashed the plane."

"It sounds like the both of you have had one hell of a night," the officer said.

"Yeah," Gary lamented, "you could say that."

Several months later, Gary learned that one of the injured men died in the hospital. He never did find out if it was the man that flew with him or Jack. Perhaps it was better that way.

Chapter Sixteen

The Boy Who Wandered Off

Something didn't feel right. Warden Dennis McIntosh sat along the edge of a pool on the Stroudwater River in Gorham, prepping for the dive. He was in a full-body wetsuit that went over his head, an oxygen tank strapped to his back, and the face mask with breathing apparatus in place. It was early March, and the Gorham Country Club fairway that led to the river before him and the putting green behind, was half-covered in snow, areas of dead grass showing where the sun touched most. Except, this Saturday morning was shrouded in cloud cover, and gentle snowflakes drifted down from the sky, which cast everything in a low, gray light.

Dennis looked down to his left. There, in the snow, were the footprints of a six-year-old boy named Andy, who came to explore the river. It was something he'd probably done a hundred times before. Perhaps his parents had brought him here in the summer to look for frogs and salamanders. Maybe they'd gone fishing. Andy's home wasn't far away, a short walk through the adjacent woods and game preserve. He'd gone outside to play with his older sister the afternoon before, and after a brief period, his parents noticed he was missing. They found Andy's tracks leading into the woods, and when it started getting dark, they called the authorities.

Hundreds of personnel answered the call, including wardens, state and local police, firemen, and volunteers, all of whom scoured the area overnight.

The only trace of Andy was a set of tracks leading to the open pool. No doubt curious and excited as he made his way across the slightly sloped putting green, Andy was innocent of the dangers before him. The rest of the story was told in the snow. There was a thin streak on the bank where his foot slipped, exposing ice underneath, and an impression where he'd landed on his butt and slid into the water. What likely happened next is too horrific for any parent to imagine.

Andy had gone into the water and he didn't get out—that much was a near certainty. There was only one set of tracks leading to the open pool, the rest of the river was covered with ice, and trained canines had gone up and down the riverbank several times over without detecting Andy's scent. Now, it was Dennis's job to find the boy's body. That was the deal. There was no such thing as search and rescue for the dive team. Every year, far too many people go into Maine's lakes, ponds, rivers, and streams without coming out, and it's up to the divers to bring them back. Dennis had gone on countless dives before, and on a few occasions, he'd been the one to find the missing person, to come face-to-face in the murky water with a bloated corpse. Experience didn't exactly make the job easier. On this morning, there was a gnawing pit in Dennis's stomach. All he kept thinking was that the boy should be home watching Saturday morning cartoons. If Dennis waited just a little longer, maybe word would come that Andy was found hiding in his parents' basement.

A helicopter equipped with a heat-seeking device passed overhead. The churning beat of the rotors returned Dennis's thoughts to reality. There wouldn't be a happy ending today.

Dennis slipped into the water.

It was a small pool, no more than twelve feet wide and four deep. Dennis started at the upstream end of the opening and paced the area. The dark water mirrored the cloud cover above, preventing him from seeing anything without going under. He was in to his waist and the current was formidable, pushing against his thighs and creating an eddy on his downstream side. Taking short, careful steps (he wasn't wearing flippers), his feet slipped in and around the many rocks on the bottom. At the edge of the ice, Dennis dove under to investigate the river bank, where overhangs and roots could have entrapped the boy. Several passes back and forth returned no sign of Andy.

Dennis continued through the middle of the pool, the water up to his chest. Andy had slipped in at this spot, so it was most likely the body would be found at the downstream end. Several times Dennis kicked something on the bottom worth taking a look at, but all he found were rocks with a collection of sticks, leaves, and golf balls stuck around them. He made a complete sweep of the pool without finding Andy or any sign of the boy. Dennis knew not to get his hopes up. This could only mean one thing, and it wasn't good.

Several wardens helped Dennis from the pool. He took off the face mask and looked up at Don Gray, the supervising warden.

"The boy's not in there," Dennis said, "and there's only one way out."

"How's the current?" Don asked.

"Strong enough to pull a small child under the ice, I'm afraid." Dennis took a deep breath. "The ice is six inches to a foot thick at the outlet, and the water flowing out is, at least, two feet deep."

"Okay, thanks," Don said. "I was hoping it wouldn't come to this, but I placed a few calls earlier just in case. We're going to get an excavator in here to break up the river ice."

Dennis went back to his truck and changed out of the wetsuit and into his warden uniform. On his way back, he passed a table of donuts, sandwiches, and coffee donated by local businesses. Most of the on-duty personnel, himself included, had been on the scene overnight, and if there's anything positive to take from a tragedy such as this, it's that the community rises to the occasion and comes to their aid. Dennis wasn't feeling up to food, but there was an exhausted, ghost-like trance overcoming him, so he grabbed a coffee and sipped it black.

It was two hours before the excavator arrived, during which they milled around, waiting. The food disappeared and Dennis floated from one empty conversation to another. Nobody wanted to talk on a day like this, but they had to pass the time, and so there seemed to be a playbook of things people said to get them through. When the excavator arrived, Dennis found himself at the riverside in one of these conversations with a volunteer fireman named Scott.

"What a shame," Scott said. "Something like this. I can't imagine what the parents are going through."

"It's tragic," Dennis agreed.

"I've got kids," Scott said. "A boy and a girl, just like them, both not much older than this boy. It makes you think, you know?"

"It sure does."

All conversation stopped as the excavator dug into the frozen river at the edge of the pool. A loud crack preceded a large slab of ice being raised into the air and flipped over to expose the underside. There was no sign of Andy, and so the excavator went in for a second scoop.

"Do you have kids?" Scott asked.

"I do. Four girls, all much older. The youngest is in high school now. I can tell you that you never stop asking that question."

"Which question?"

The excavator raised another slab.

"What if?" Dennis said, his voice trailing off as he inspected the ice.

Nothing.

The operator continued to work the excavator down the river, each bucket load affecting the ebb and flow of conversation. After a couple of hours and approximately 250 yards of uncovered river, the excavator closed in on a concrete, cart-path bridge, beyond which was all forest. Heads were shaking in frustration with each unsuccessful scoop, the wardens beginning to exchange knowing glances.

"What happens if the excavator gets to the bridge without finding the boy?" Scott asked.

"That's a good question," Dennis said. "It won't be able to go into the woods. We'll probably break the ice underneath the bridge by hand, but by that point it will be getting dark, so we'll have to suspend the search."

"Until tomorrow?"

"Not likely. It's not my call, but there's a good chance we postpone until the ice melts."

"Are you serious?"

"Unfortunately, yes. There's not much more we can do here. Breaking the ice by hand will be extremely time-consuming and costly. There's no question the boy is deceased at this point so it will be more prudent to wait."

They watched as the excavator went in for one last dig before the bridge. It raised a large slab of ice that extended beyond the bucket's jaws. A hush came over the onlookers as they all realized that something blue was on the underside. Dennis's breath escaped him and his body was suddenly cemented in place. It was Andy.

His blue winter coat and matching snow pants frozen to the ice. The excavator jerked, and from ten feet up, Andy fell to the ground.

Scott rushed to the boy and Dennis followed. Scooping the body up from the ground, Scott placed Andy in Dennis's outstretched arms. All color was drained from Andy's face, leaving an angelic white complexion that was framed by a golden crown of blond hair matted to his forehead. Andy's mouth was agape, his wide eyes a brilliant, sparkling blue as if he was frozen in childhood wonder. It was an expression Dennis recognized from his daughters—that brief pause on Christmas morning, a new discovery preceding a shriek of joy. Only Andy's appearance reflected the horrific moment curiosity escaped him, passing from this world to the next.

The weight of Andy's body failed to register in Dennis's grasp. The boy seemed to float before him as Dennis shuffled toward the emergency vehicles. Several people spoke to him, their voices heard but the words lost. Open hands appeared before Dennis. Without taking note of who it was, he placed Andy into the outstretched arms of another green warden uniform. In doing so, he passed the burden of memory, the promise in Andy's blue eyes left to strike a chord in another. How many people would walk away from this day unable to forget the boy who wandered off?

Dennis stumbled from the scene.

"Sergeant McIntosh," a woman called to him. Dennis recognized her as a reporter for the *Portland Press Herald*. "May I have a word?"

He nodded.

"Where was the boy found?"

Dennis explained that an excavator operator retrieved the boy from under the river ice. He went on to talk about the dangers of spring ice on all of Maine's waters. He made his way to his truck.

Exhausted from being on the search for over twenty-four hours, along with the mental fatigue, the drive home was slow going. Each time Dennis glanced at the speedometer, he was well below the speed limit, a line of headlights growing in his rearview mirror. It was early evening when Dennis pulled into his driveway. He sat in the truck for a moment, his thoughts continuing to fall on the boy.

Dennis's wife, Carmen, was at the kitchen sink doing dishes when he came through the front door.

"Did you find the boy?" she asked over her shoulder.

His legs began to tremble and his knees gave way. Dennis fell back against the door and he slid to the floor. He could still feel Andy's nylon coat in his hands as he covered his face, tears coursing into his palms.

Chapter Seventeen

The Undercover Warden

"Let's say we catch someone tonight," Warden Glynn Pratt said as he brushed a blade of grass from his face. Along with Garrett McPherson and Mike Marshall, the three wardens were lying in the foot-deep grass of an open field on a cold and moonless November night. "To get a conviction from an honorable judge of Washington County, we'll have to nab the guy red-handed—literally, elbows deep, field-dressing the deer, blood all over his arms."

"Don't forget his clothes," Garrett said. He was several feet away on Glynn's right, but it was so dark out that Glynn couldn't see him.

"What about them?"

"Where have you been, Pratt? I thought everyone knew this. To get a conviction in the county, you have to submit no less than five articles of clothing with evidence on it. I'm talking coat, pants, long johns, underwear, and, at least, one sock. Preferably the left one."

"That's what I heard," Mike said from his hiding spot on the other side of Glynn. He, too, was hidden in the darkness. "Except Garrett is missing the fact that the poacher's name also has to be written on the tag of his underwear by his mother. It's inadmissible if anyone else writes it, so handwriting analysis will be needed."

Nobody knows exactly which judge said it, or who was on the receiving end, but, legend has it that one judge looked down his nose at a warden in court and decreed: "Poaching is not a crime in Washington County; it's a way of life."

Glynn believed the legend without hesitation. After all, the judge was right. Poaching *had been* an acceptable way of life in the region for many generations. Earlier wardens had knowingly turned a blind eye to Down East poaching because the area's economic challenges made it a necessity for survival. Those were tough times before the inception of welfare programs. That was no longer the case. Public assistance was readily available for those in need, making night hunting indefensible. If only the judges would catch up. The best a warden could do in Washington County in the late 1970s, it so often seemed, was cross his *t*'s, dot his *i*'s, and bury his frustration in jest.

"You know," Glynn said. "To some degree, I can't blame a local judge that snickers at gaming laws. I sometimes feel foolish in court when I'm bringing a fishing violation before a judge who just presided over a domestic assault case."

"Me too," Garrett said. "Which is another reason why we have to present irrefutable evidence to move our cases along, and we're forgetting the most important detail."

Glynn took the bait. "What's that?"

"So far we've only proven that our hypothetical poacher was caught field dressing a deer after dark. No self-respecting county judge is going to convict someone on that alone. It is hunting season. How do we prove he didn't shoot the deer during the day?"

"I've got a foot-long thermometer in the truck that will prove it," Glynn said.

"And you know exactly where the judge will tell you to stick that thermometer," Garrett shot back. "What we need is visual evidence."

"Like a Polaroid?"

"You got it. Taken at the exact moment the rifle is fired."

"But no flash photography," Mike said.

"Of course not," Glynn said. "Lighting a field at night is illegal. The judge is more likely to fine *us*."

The three men were quiet for a moment. Glynn blew on his hands to warm his fingertips as he took stock of their situation. The temperature had dropped to the dew point; no doubt a frost would be forming on the damp grass soon. It was so dark out that he couldn't see anything past the blades of grass that kept tickling his face.

"We're out of luck tonight," Mike said.

"Yep," Glynn replied. "It's a good night to be a poacher."

Mike's radio crackled. The State Police barracks received a call from a South Princeton resident who had heard gunshots in his field. The shots were fired around nine o'clock, about a half hour ago, and the local hadn't seen or heard anything since. The suspect could still be there.

"Looks like we've got the right night, but the wrong field," Mike said after ending his conversation with the State Police. "Let's go check it out."

"What's the point?" Glynn said. "We weren't there to get the Polaroid."

Garrett laughed. "That's true. But the one thing in Washington County that's harder to get than a judge's conviction is a poaching tip from the public. Who knows? Maybe it's our lucky night?"

The three of them went back to their trucks. Glynn and Garrett were familiar with the field in question. It was large, a quarter of a mile in length, with fifty to seventy-five yards open to the road. The complainant's house was located at the front corner, and because it was a calm and quiet night, they knew driving there would risk alerting the perpetrator to their presence. They decided they'd all ride in Mike's truck to within a mile of the field. Glynn and Garrett would then jump out and run to the house while Mike drove an intersecting road in search of any vehicles. It was possible the poacher could have parked along the other road and approached the field through the woods.

It was around 10:30 when Glynn and Garrett arrived at the house.

"Good," the man who opened the door said, "you're here." He eagerly extended his hand to shake. "Earl Thomas, but folks call me E.T." Likely in his early forties and tall enough that he had to duck under the door frame, E.T. was already dressed in a bright blue parka and about to step out the door into the cold.

"Sir," Glynn said, "you can't go out there with us."

"Oh, I know. I'm in my warm clothes because I've been doing a little recon from the back porch."

"Did you see or hear anything else?" Garrett asked.

"There haven't been any more shots, but I swear I saw a flicker of light in the back corner of the field. It was real quick—as if to check something."

"What about vehicles?" Glynn asked.

"Traffic is rare out here at night, so we typically notice when a car passes, but to my knowledge, no one has come by."

"Okay, thanks," Glynn said. "We're going to have to ask you to stay in the house. Lock the doors and don't do anything that could attract the attention of whoever's out there. Keep the dog inside if you have one, and don't turn on the back light, slam the house door, start the car, etcetera. We'll let you know when we're done."

"Roger that," E.T. said with a smile.

The two wardens split up to check the field; Garrett would walk the tree line closest to the house and Glynn would do the same on the far side of the field. Glynn slowly made his way along the groove of a tractor path in the same way a hunter would looking for deer—take a step, stop, listen, repeat. Over the course of his two years in the Warden Service, Glynn had honed his night-time observation skills, but as dark as it was on this evening, it didn't really matter how well his eyes adjusted. He couldn't see anything past the reach of his arms, making it one of those times he had to be all ears. It was a good night for listening, at least. There was no wind to muffle sounds and rustle the last of fall's leaves. The only thing he could hear was the occasional hoot of an owl that was probably a mile away.

Glynn was about two-thirds of the way down the field when a stick cracked in the woods at a ten-o'clock position to him. He froze, listening, but nothing stirred.

When he'd worked the same field before with Garrett, he remembered there was an old logging road not too far into the woods that ran parallel to the field. That previous experience had been a long and fruitless night, but maybe it would aid him now. There was no way he'd be able to reach the road without making a sound by going through the woods, so he turned around and made his way back.

From the main road, Glynn re-entered the woods via the logging road. To avoid making a sound, the going was even slower than it had been in the field, but that didn't matter to Glynn. He may have only been a warden for two years, but he'd already spent countless nights hiding in bushes and lying in fields, and, more times than he'd care to admit, the only thing he'd caught was the shivers. The possibility of being on the cusp of a bust had him suddenly sweating. Each step was bringing him one step closer to whoever broke that stick. But after a while, it seemed to be taking forever. How far had he gone? And shouldn't he have reached the poacher by now? What if the sound he heard was actually a man making his way *to* the field? If that were the case, he'd just cleared the path and the guy was getting away. He couldn't be in two places at once, but Glynn didn't know if his instinct had led him toward or astray from finally catching a poacher.

Another stick broke. It was on the road, not far ahead. Glynn squatted close to the ground to make himself as small and invisible as possible. The soft padding of footsteps on damp leaves came into range. Coming closer and closer. He'd wait until it got to within five or six feet and then quickly rush the poacher—Glynn just hoped it wasn't a bear. His heart was off to the races and he was doing all he could to conceal his breathing. There it was again. A small twig snapped. Ten yards away. He planted his left hand into the muddy earth and knuckled the ground with his Kel-Lite in the other, ready to explode like a sprinter from the blocks. The time was now.

Glynn burst from the ground. He took two strides, flicked on his Kel-Light, and yelled, "Warden Service, hold it right there!" A blur of blue movement flashed before him. He grabbed a fistful of nylon jacket. The man spun. Glynn lost his grip and stumbled over something long and dense on the ground. Another man brushed past him. Glynn gave chase into the woods, trying to keep his light on the suspects. They split up and Glynn followed the man closest to him, which was the guy he'd grabbed before. Holding his forearms up in an attempt to block the branches scraping his face, Glynn bowled through the thicket. Off to his left, the second suspect swore and crashed to the ground. Glynn continued on, and when he finally broke into the field, the first suspect was a good twenty yards ahead.

"Stop!" Glynn yelled, shining his light at the man's back. His command was ignored. Then, out of the darkness, Garrett sprinted through the beam of Glynn's light and launched himself at the man's chest. The suspect's feet flipped into the air.

"There's a second suspect in the woods," Glynn yelled to Garrett. "I think I can flush him out."

"Let's secure this guy first," Garrett replied.

"Be right there," Glynn yelled. Garrett had a decade of warden experience under his belt, so Glynn trusted his judgment.

The tackled suspect was young, no older than mid-twenties. He wasn't saying anything, but they assumed his accomplice was of similar age. This could be good, and bad. On one hand, they weren't dealing with crafty, tight-lipped old timers who knew the tricks of the poaching trade. On the other hand, their youthfulness made them unpredictable, not to mention harder to catch in a foot race. Glynn helped Garrett pick the first suspect off the ground and handcuffed him to a tree. Glynn started working his way down the tree line toward where he had heard the other suspect fall. Garrett moved back into the field a bit to cut the suspect off if he ran.

The light Glynn cast into the trees shone on several large maples and a bunch of small whips. They were mostly bare of leaves, which should help in spotting the guy. He had to be in there somewhere; otherwise, they would have heard him flee. And then he did. Flushed from the tree line like partridge from cover, the second suspect broke into the field at a full sprint. Glynn was thirty yards behind him from the get-go, and as fast as the guy appeared to be, the chances of running him down were slim. Hopefully, Garrett was in a good position to cut him off.

"Don't mess with him," Glynn yelled as loud as he could. "Take him out!"

All of a sudden the suspect stopped and threw up his arms. "Don't shoot!" he shouted. "Please don't shoot!" He was visibly shaking beneath his red winter coat.

Glynn had only meant for Garrett to tackle the man, but if he was going to turn himself in out of fear of being shot—well, that worked, too. They quickly handcuffed the second suspect and brought him back to where they'd left his buddy. Seeing both men together and checking their IDs, Glynn realized they were brothers. They'd never been busted before, but Glynn recognized the family name from poaching rumors exchanged through the wardens. Their clan was partly responsible for when Glynn and Garrett had worked this field the first time. This would be an important bust for curbing their illicit activity. There was just one problem: they didn't have any evidence. There was what appeared to be blood around the cuffs of the first suspect's blue coat, but without a deer and a gun, it wouldn't be nearly enough. It was time for the good-cop, bad-cop routine.

Glynn got in the face of the first suspect, a slender young man with a mustache who he now knew was twenty-two years old. "Where is it?" Glynn demanded without stating exactly what "it" was. "What did you do with it?"

"You dumb son of a bitch," the first suspect said.

His younger brother's eyes widened. The second suspect was only nineteen, and clearly still fearful of being shot.

"You must be blind as a fuckin' bat," the older brother continued. "You tripped over the damn thing."

He was right. They must have dropped the rifle and left the deer where Glynn initially jumped them. At the time Glynn was so focused on the men, he hadn't even looked at what he tripped over. The wardens led the men back through the woods to the logging road. Sure enough, they found a handsome eight-point buck at the point of initial contact. It was fully dressed and still steaming, so it was obvious the deer hadn't been killed before nightfall. A few feet away was a Remington .30-06 rifle with a scope. Now they had all three pieces to the conviction puzzle.

Garrett called Mike on his two-way radio and informed him that they'd need a pick-up. They had two men with reservations at the Calais Police Department.

As they loaded the brothers into the truck, it occurred to Glynn that if they were on foot, then someone would have to be picking them up. Glynn did a double-take of the older brother's jacket. He was wearing a blue coat nearly identical to the one E.T. had on.

"I have an idea," he said to Garrett and Mike. He took the ball cap from the older brother, a black hat with an orange Stihl logo, and put it on his own head. Glynn then ran back to the house and knocked on the door. "We've got the guys," he said when E.T. answered. "Mind if I borrow your coat."

"Eh—"

"I'm going undercover," he told E.T. "To see if I can catch the pickup driver. I'll leave my coat here as collateral."

"In that case, it's all yours."

E.T.'s coat was big on him, but it was good enough to create the ruse. While Mike drove the brothers to jail, Glynn and Garrett dragged the deer to the roadside. Garrett hid behind an oak tree while Glynn crouched next to the deer. Ten minutes later, a vehicle approached. Glynn flashed his light to signal it. An old brown Scout truck pulled up and the driver hopped out while leaving the engine idling. Glynn turned his back to the driver and tried his best to mimic the older brother's voice.

"Gimme a hand," he said.

The man shined his light on the deer for a moment, and then he redirected it to Glynn.

"Hell no!" the man spat. He ran back to the truck and sped out of there as fast as his rust bucket on wheels could go.

"That almost worked," Garrett said, coming out from behind the tree. He shined his light on Glynn's uniform pants. "The black stripe gave you away."

"Yeah, these pants make quite the fashion statement, don't they? Oh well, nothing ventured, nothing gained."

There was no point in going after the Scout truck. They couldn't arrest the driver for stopping to look, so they had a local police officer bring them to the Calais Police Department, where the two brothers were waiting in a holding cell. The wardens took no chances with evidence collection, bagging and tagging every piece of clothing that had deer hair or blood on it. By the end of it, the older brother walked out of the building wearing nothing more than his underwear and socks.

The driver of the Scout truck was waiting in the parking lot. He was looking over the deer in the back of Mike's truck.

"Look at that," the man yelled to the boys. "A perfect kill shot. I'm proud of ya!"

Glynn shook his head as they drove away. "Some people just don't learn."

"I don't know about that," Mike said. "On the ride to the jail, the younger brother asked me if wardens can shoot people. I told him it depended on the circumstances, which is why they issue us guns. And then he said, 'I think I saved my life tonight.'"

Glynn laughed. "Not quite, but I suppose it can't hurt if he thinks that. Maybe he'll stick to legal hunting from now on."

On their day in court, the brothers pleaded guilty and were convicted. This in itself was a surprise to the wardens.

Chapter Eighteen

Rolfe Brook Smelt Run

Nat Berry crouched behind a fallen tree. Everything was wet from the spring melt, and the cold ground sparked a shiver. Three men had emerged on the bank of Rolfe Brook in Raymond, a popular stream for smelters and those simply out to catch a glimpse of the fish's annual migration. The brook had been closed to smelting for as long as anyone could remember, but the fifty-dollar fine wasn't enough to deter everyone interested in more than sightseeing. The trick was figuring out who was who.

Each of the men carried a beer, which alone wasn't suspicious; however, if any of them so much as scooped a smelt into a can, they wouldn't be the first to be pinched for it. The telltale sign they were up to no good was how they fanned out to case the area. They knew to look for wardens before dipping into the brook, essentially turning the situation into a backwoods game of hide and seek.

A short man with a rugged build came toward Nat. He weaved around the sporadic patches of snow as he scanned the area like a prison night watchman, going so far as to shine his flashlight up trees with branches low enough to climb. The closer he got, the more it felt like Nat's heart was going to beat out of his chest. It only stood to reason that if he could see this man, then the man could see him. The smelter stopped and looked back at his buddies, and for a moment, it appeared as though he was going to head back to the brook. No such luck. He continued on until the glow of his flashlight was shining off Nat's well-polished black boots. Perhaps this was why Russ Dyer always chided Nat for being too clean. Nat held his breath, waiting for the man to say something. Instead, there was the unmistakable sound of a zipper, followed by a grunt. Nat had suddenly found himself a front-row spectator to nature's calling. He kept his head down, doing his best to avoid flinching as piddle spatter ricocheted onto his boots. The man groaned and the stream intensified. Dear God, was it ever going to stop? This guy's body held beer better than a camel. When the man finally finished, he zipped up and turned back to the brook.

"All clear over here," he yelled to his buddies.

Nat couldn't help but smile. Sure, he'd have to polish his boots again, but he was going to do that tomorrow anyway. Through the trees, he could see the flashlights from the other two men circling back, which meant wardens Don Gray and Grant Casey also went unfound. If this was indeed a game of hide and seek, the good guys were about win. The smelters regrouped at the stream, and one man ducked into the bushes and out of sight, returning a few minutes later with three five-gallon buckets. They shined their lights on the water and hooted in admiration at the fish. Wasting no time, the man who marked his territory in front of Nat dipped a long-handled net into the water while the other two waited with the buckets. The net was nearly full when it came out of the water, a shimmering, writhing, silver mass of finger-sized fish. Nat waited. At the rate the men were shoveling smelts into buckets, they'd be ready to split in a couple minutes—tops. Nat's view was partially obstructed by a large pine, and he wanted to make sure the third man had fish in his bucket so that all three were implicated before revealing himself.

Grant acted first. "That'll be enough," he announced.

The three men stopped what they were doing and slowly stood.

"Well, if it isn't Dale Murphy," Nat said, coming out of his hiding spot. Dale was the oldest brother in a family well known to the wardens. "You almost got me back there."

"Nat," Dale said, "had I known you were in there, I would have drank more beer and aimed higher."

"Don't I know it. I see you've brought Bobby and Mike. The whole family is here. Good evening, gentlemen."

"It was good," Bobby, the youngest of the Murphy brothers, said. "Before you guys showed up."

"Sorry to ruin your fun," Grant said, "but that's what the governor pays us for."

"I had a feeling you'd be out tonight," Dale said. "That's why I brought this." He reached into his back pocket and pulled out his checkbook. "Fifty bucks a head if I'm not mistaken. I can still pay you here, can't I?"

"Sure," Nat said. "You just need to sign the paperwork that says you're guilty."

"Hell," Dale scoffed. "We all know these fish didn't jump in the pails by themselves."

"Nat," Don said, arriving on the scene. He'd been hiding further downstream. "Why don't you and Grant take these guys out to Russ for processing? I'll stick around here in case any more customers come along."

Don was the supervising warden, so Nat and Grant did as he requested, leading the Murphy brothers out to the Plains Road and then down to Route 121, where Russ Dyer was parked in a department truck. They hurried the paperwork along as fast as they could, and to save time on the return trip, Nat and Grant cut through the woods. The wardens emerged about a hundred feet from the brook and were stepping through what remained of the plowed snow bank on the Plains Road when they heard Don yelling.

"Hold it! Game warden!"

A car engine roared. The vehicle spun out in the dirt for a second before screeching onto the pavement. The car's lights were off as it drove diagonally across the road, directly at Nat and Grant.

"Get the plate!" Nat yelled to Grant. "I'll go for the windshield!"

Grant shouted out the license plate number as Nat threw his Kel-Lite at the windshield. There was a loud smashing sound at the exact moment the car's headlights came on. Nat was blinded by the light and he instinctively raised his arms to shield his face. The car swerved at the last moment, splashing slush up onto the snow bank and its occupants. It sped away, leaving in its wake the clanking sound of Nat's flashlight hitting the pavement.

Nat went to retrieve his busted flashlight while Grant shined his light toward where the car originated. There appeared to be a man lying face-down on the ground. Was Don hit by the car? The wardens sprinted to his aid, but as they got closer, it became clear that the man on the ground was wearing jeans and a flannel jacket instead of a warden's uniform. His arms were also pinned behind his back and he was in handcuffs.

"This fellow here wanted to wrestle," came a voice from the shadows. Don was standing off the road with one hand propped against a birch tree. "Guess who won?"

"That doesn't seem like a fair fight," Nat said. "Did you tell him you have a black belt in judo?"

"Might not have mentioned it."

"Figures," the man on the ground spat.

"Oh," Don said. "Look who's talking? Are you ready to tell us who was driving the car?"

"What car?"

"The brown Chevy Impala," Grant said. "Looked to be a '65. Plate number G364YM7."

"I don't know."

"Look, numbnuts," Don said, "we've got the make, model, and plate. Unless the car is registered to you, we're going to catch him, so why don't you play nice?"

"Like I said, I don't know."

"This is BS. Let's PR this guy on top of Black Cat Mountain," Grant said, referring to a personal recognizance document. If the man signed it, they could release him then and there under the agreement that he would appear in court. Failure to do so would result in jail time and a hefty fine.

"I don't know," Don said. "Seems like a lot of work for a fifty-dollar fine."

"Wait—what?" the man said. "Are you serious? All of this was over a fifty-dollar fine?"

"It was," Don said. "You're going to be on the books for the sparring session, too. I have to warn you, my lessons aren't cheap."

The next day, Nat looked up the plate number, and after a few follow-up phone calls, he discovered that the car's owner worked at a lumberyard in Naples. Don was in the Gray office so the two of them took a ride out to investigate. The employee parking lot was located on the opposite side of Route 302 from the lumberyard. In the front row, they found a brown Chevy Impala with a softball-sized indent in the windshield where the rearview mirror should have been. The entire windshield was spider webbed.

"Nice shot," Don said.

"Being lefty gave me a pretty good angle," Nat told him.

"I always knew you weren't right."

Nat laughed. "What do you say we go down to the lumberyard and talk to this guy?"

"I don't know." Don stared at the car while rapping his knuckles on the passenger window. "After fleeing last night, what are the odds he comes clean today? We don't have any evidence that he was the one driving. He'll probably tell us the windshield was fine when he came to work this morning. It seems like a lot of hassle for fifty dollars."

"We can get him for resisting arrest and driving to endanger, too."

"Sure, if we can prove he was the one driving, which we can't." Don pointed at the car. "Look at that thing. It's going to cost him at least three hundred to get the windshield replaced. I'd say he's paid his fine right there."

"That's true," Nat agreed. "He'll be into it even deeper if the police catch him operating the car like that. I wonder how he can even see the road?"

"You know, that's an interesting idea."

"Are you thinking what I'm thinking?"

"Yep. Let's give the State Police a call. They can surprise him on his way home."

Chapter Nineteen

Better Luck Next Year

"I just received a tip," Jim Brown said over the phone to Nat Berry. "Someone I know by the name of Gee Bennett. Good guy, I trust him. Anyway, Gee lives out in Durham, and he said a shot was fired into the field across the street from his house around ten tonight."

"That was just a half hour ago," Nat said.

"Yep, Gee called me right away. There's more. . . ." Jim paused to catch his breath. "He saw a truck leave the scene."

"You think it's him?"

"Might be."

"Well then, what are we waiting for?"

Him. The two wardens didn't have to say the name Danny James to know who they were discussing. The poacher's notoriety had grown to local-legend status, to the point of which all suspected illegal hunting was attributed to Danny, whether he was involved or not. People just assumed, and for good reason. Despite his increasingly brazen activity and several close calls, Danny had never been caught. So it stood to reason that if shots were fired at night, or out of season, and there were no arrests, then it had to be *him.* Most of Danny's alleged activity occurred in Jim and Nat's districts, pitting the wardens against him in a long-running game of cat and mouse. Danny, a part-time lobsterman and clam digger from Yarmouth, wasn't shy about pointing to the scoreboard in his not so subtle ways. One day Jim found his mailbox stuffed with rotting herring, a fish commonly used as lobster bait. No doubt, it was *him*. To top it off, during the previous holiday season, both Jim and Nat received Christmas cards in the mail with no return address. The only thing written inside was the message, "Better luck next year!"

As far as Jim and Nat were concerned, Danny was at the top—and bottom—of Yarmouth, Maine's most-wanted list. So when Gee called Jim late on a cold November night in 1980, they pursued the tip without question or hesitation. Jim picked up Nat on the way to Gee's residence, an old white farmhouse situated atop a hill at the corner of a three-way intersection. The house's black front door swung open as they drove up the long driveway. A white-haired man dressed in overalls and an unzipped wool coat strode across the porch.

"That's Gee," Jim said. "He's a bit of a character."

"I heard a shot fired into the field across the street," Gee said in a husky voice. A dog was barking wildly inside the house, which Gee dispatched with one shout over his shoulder. He then leaned in and rested his forearms on the back of Jim's truck as he continued to speak. "Got to the window just in time to see a truck drive away."

"How many shots were fired?" Jim asked.

"Just the one."

"Can you describe the truck?" Nat asked.

"Easy there, fella," Gee said. "I may look spry as a kitten, but these old bones don't move like they used to. By the time I got to the window, all I saw were taillights. I s'pose it was full size."

The sound of a large puttering engine permeated the darkness.

Headlights crested the hill. Jim's truck was behind a thick row of lilac bushes where it was unlikely to be seen from the road. This obstruction also meant they weren't in a good position to see, so the three of them ducked into the lilac bushes to get a better view. They were only about twenty feet from the road as a large truck came down the hill and slowly drove by the field. It was suspicious, to say the least. Even more so because it appeared to be a white Ford F-150, a truck well known to Jim and Nat.

"Was that the truck?" Jim asked.

"Might be," Gee said. "Taillights look familiar."

"You recognize it?" Jim said to Nat.

"Sure do," Nat said. "That's *him.*"

"Him who?" Gee wanted to know.

"Can't tell you that right now," Jim said. "But we've been after this guy for a while now, and if we catch him tonight, you'll be the first to know. If you don't mind, Nat and I will be spending the evening staking out the field from your property."

"Mind? It's why I called." Gee checked his watch. "Look at that, it's almost midnight. Way past my bedtime. If you boys don't mind, I'm going to turn in. Happy hunting."

"Don't forget to lock the doors," Jim said.

Gee waved the notion away with his hand. "If the dog don't get 'em, I keep a guard shotgun next to the bed just in case."

Once Gee was inside, the wardens covered Jim's truck with a parachute and snuck into the field to look for evidence. They'd never be able to prove that Danny fired the shot unless he killed a deer. Only one shot was fired, but they knew enough of Danny's track record to have faith in his marksmanship. The fact he drove by the field an hour after the initial shot suggested Danny believed he'd hit his target, too.

Starting in the center of the field, they each took a side and canvassed their zone in a zigzag pattern. It was close enough to a full moon that Jim could see without a flashlight. He slowly worked his way through the hayfield's leftover, knee-deep grass. A half hour passed without a single reason to turn on his light. It wasn't until his final pass along the tree line that he came to a dark figure lying in the grass. Jim turned on his light to find a dead doe at his feet.

He yelled to Nat.

"We're going to get *him*," Jim proclaimed when Nat arrived. "We're finally gonna nab this SOB." Jim took out his pocket knife and cut a small wedge about a half inch wide out of the deer's ear, which he tucked into his breast pocket for safekeeping.

"Lights," Nat said, pointing to the road. Both wardens quickly shut off their flashlights and dropped into the grass. A vehicle came slowly down the hill from the same direction the previous truck had come earlier, turning right at the three-way intersection just as the truck had done.

"That looked like Danny's other vehicle, the sedan," Nat said once the car disappeared.

"I believe it's a four-door, maroon Pontiac." Jim checked his watch. "Makes sense. It's about a half-hour drive from here to his house, and it's been an hour since the truck drove by."

The wardens left the deer and went back to hide in the lilac bushes near the house. They were careful to walk in separate, meandering paths so as to avoid creating the appearance of a trail in the grass. The lilacs offered good cover and a perfect vantage point of the hill. They were a little further away from the deer than what they may have liked—it was out of sight in the grass—but once Danny got his hands on the doe, they'd easily be able to sneak into the field and cut him off before he reached his vehicle. Or so they thought.

"This will be just perfect," Nat whispered, "if we catch him on an informant's tip."

"Why does that matter?" Jim asked.

"Didn't I tell you about the run-in we had where he accused me of threatening him?" Nat said.

"Not sure."

"I saw him one day parked along a field over in New Glouces-ter, not far from the warden station. I could only imagine what he was up to. He was just standing there next to the road looking into the field, so I stopped to ask what he was looking at.

"Nothing really," he said. "Just looking. I like fields."

"It was obvious he was BS-ing me, so I said to him, 'You know, Danny, there are a lot of people who don't like what you've been doing. Sooner or later one of these landowners is going to do something about it. They're going to get you.'

"A week later the Sergeant calls me into his office. Tells me he got a call from Danny's lawyer, who accused me of threatening his client. Said I told Danny that I was going to get him."

"Typical Danny," Jim said. "What a weasel."

Headlights once again crested the hill. This time, it was the white F-150 that drove by at a parade pace. There appeared to be a second person sitting on the passenger side. Jim checked the time. It had been an hour since the Pontiac passed.

"What do you want to bet the car comes by in another hour?" Jim asked.

"No bet," Nat replied.

"He's not driving off the road onto the shoulder. Nor did I see any tracks in the dirt when we crossed the road. He knew not to leave any trace, and now they're probably looking to see if we've pulled over to investigate."

"There's a reason we haven't caught him yet."

"I hate to admit it, but he's smart."

"The good news is he mustn't know we're here, otherwise, why would he keep coming by?"

"This is going to be fun."

Jim was correct; the Pontiac reappeared an hour later. Then the truck an hour after that. The pattern continued until daybreak when the white F-150 parked just past the end of the field where the power lines came out. Three men dressed in hunter-orange vests got out and began working their way down the power lines. About fifty yards of woods stood between the power lines and the field, so once the hunters got away from the road they were out of sight. It wasn't long, however, until the orange vests reappeared in the woods behind the deer. Jim and Nat agreed to wait until they grabbed the deer before apprehending them. The thing was, the orange vests didn't approach the deer. They loitered in the woods behind it for quite some time, and at one point even moved beyond the deer.

"What are they doing?" Jim asked. He kept switching his weight from one knee to the other, finding it difficult to stay still, the anticipation killing him. "Why aren't they getting the deer?"

"I don't know," Nat said. "It looks as if they're actually hunting."

The orange vests continued to move into the woods away from the deer and eventually were out of sight.

"I don't get it," Jim said. "Do you think they saw our footprints near the deer?"

"Not likely. They never went to the edge of the field."

"But they must have seen the deer, they were within fifteen feet of it. I doubt it was a coincidence they spent that much time directly behind the deer without knowing it was there."

"I agree," Nat said. "Maybe they're making sure no one else is around?"

The sound of a vehicle starting caught Jim's attention. He looked to Danny's truck in time to see the white F-150 drive away.

"I don't believe it," Jim said. "Where are they going?"

"Maybe they'll come back?"

After an hour of waiting, the wardens decided to check on the deer. By this point, if Danny was coming back, it probably was going to be after dark. They went to the opposite end of the field from where the truck had parked and worked their way along the tree line, only to discover the deer was gone.

"What the—" Jim was distracted by drag marks in the pine needles leading into the woods. Then it hit him. "They took the vests off. They took the vests off and snuck in to get the deer. We were looking for orange the whole time, so we never saw them."

"I bet when they moved beyond the deer as if they were hunting, they did it to draw our attention away from the deer," Nat said.

"And that's when one of them grabbed it—probably Danny, he's the shortest and hardest to see of the bunch."

"Do you think Danny knew we were here?"

"Maybe, maybe not. He probably always assumes we're after him." Jim picked up a stick and swore as he chucked it. "We were so close!"

The wardens went back to Jim's truck and removed the parachute.

"Now what?" Jim said as they climbed into the truck and he started the engine.

"Do you know if Danny has a doe permit?" Nat asked.

"He does. I looked it up earlier this season."

"I wonder if he's going to register the deer?"

"You might be onto something. Why else would he spend the entire night casing the scene, only to pull the deer out in broad daylight? Let's check the tagging stations. Maybe this time, Danny-boy will be too smart for his own good."

"Let's hope so. If not, I'm sure we'll be getting Christmas cards again this year."

The first tagging station they tried was Short Stop, a variety store on Route 9 in Pownal. The store was busy with the morning rush when they walked in, and the woman behind the counter looked to have her hands full. "I assume you want to see this," she said as they approached, handing the registration log to Jim. "Gimme a minute and I'll get you coffee."

"That'd be great, thanks," Jim said. He took one look at the top page in the log and turned to Nat. "Guess who registered a doe this morning?"

"You don't say. What town?"

"Says here our friend shot it in Pownal."

"You know," Nat said, "it's illegal to falsify a registration. We won't be able to prove he was the one who shot it, but we can get him for this and possession of a deer killed at night."

"Let's do it."

Danny had just finished hanging the deer from a tree branch when they arrived at his place in Yarmouth. From the registration log, Jim knew he hadn't bothered to weigh the doe, but it eyeballed around 140 pounds.

"That's a good-looking doe," Jim said. "Who shot it?"

"I did," Danny said. He was a short man, no taller than five feet, five inches, who looked up at Jim with a proud grin on his face.

Jim smiled right back. "Where did you shoot it?"

"In Pownal, just off the Poland Range Road."

"You don't say."

"If you'd like to see for yourself, I can take you to where we dressed it."

"I bet you can." In all likelihood, Danny had dragged the deer into the Pownal woods to gut it before going to the tagging station. He probably even fired a shot to make it look good in case anyone was in the area. "Do me a favor, can you lower the deer so I can get a look at it."

"Oh, sure," Danny said. If he was annoyed, he didn't let on. Danny appeared more than happy to display his trophy doe to the wardens. Poaching was a game to him, and in his mind, he was winning.

Jim walked around the deer and found where he'd cut a wedge out of the ear. "Hey, Danny," he said. "What do you suppose happened here?"

Danny took one look at the ear and shrugged. "I dunno."

Jim removed the wedge from his pocket. "I cut this out of a deer that was shot last night in Durham."

Danny's face went white.

"Does that look like it fits to you?" Jim said, piecing the wedge into the cut in the doe's ear.

His question was answered with a blank stare.

"I'd say it fits, so we'll be issuing you a summons. The deer and your rifle will be coming with us, which is too bad. It's a shame to waste a doe permit, but who knows, maybe you'll have better luck next year."

CHAPTER TWENTY

David Versus Goliath
(And His Chainsaw)

IT WAS A LITTLE PAST TEN ON A PERFECT JUNE NIGHT FOR A ROU-
tine patrol. Moonlight flickered through the treetops as Warden
David Berry drove the East B. Hill Road out of Andover, his left
hand hanging out the truck window to capture the breeze. Though
still early in the hiking season, Dave slowed at the Appalachian
Trail crossing just in case. Nothing stirred. He continued along
and around the next bend, he came upon a black Nissan pickup
stopped in the middle of the road. The truck's lights were on, but
there was no attempt to move as Dave turned on his emergency
lights. Saying the pickup was parked would be giving the driver too
much credit, Dave knew, because this sight was fast becoming all
too routine for his patrols.

"Oh, Stanley," Dave muttered to himself as he climbed out of
his department truck. "Now what?"

Stanley Levitt was a local millworker who liked to treat his
twelve-pack to a drive. Whether this hobby was the cause or result
of Stanley's divorce, it was hard to say. Likely a little of both. He
was obviously lonely, and it was easy to pity the guy, so on a few

previous occasions, Dave had driven Stanley home instead of arresting him for drinking and driving.

On this night, Stanley was slumped in the driver's seat, chin resting on his chest, more passed out than asleep. There was a beer bottle cradled between his legs along with several empties on the passenger-side floor. The truck was idling in neutral. All of which was a new low, even for Stanley. Dave opened the door and gently shook him awake. Stanley's head tilted ever so slightly in Dave's direction, his eyes opening no more than a slit.

"Evening, Stanley," Dave said.

Somehow, Stanley was able to muster a semi-coherent reply. "Warden."

"What are you doing here?"

"Pee."

Stanley's blue work Dickies were all wet, and judging by the smell, he hadn't spilled his beer.

"Oh, yeah," Dave said. "You know, most people get *out* to take a leak in the woods."

"I'm going."

"They also park on the side of the road, not the middle of it."

"I will."

"I think it's a little late for that."

Stanley nodded. "Home."

"Not this time, I'm afraid. You're going to have to explain this one to a judge. Now climb into the passenger seat so I can get your truck out of the road."

Stanley did as he was told, passing out again as soon as he fell into the seat. Dave parked the vehicle on the shoulder and went back to his truck to call a cruiser for pickup. A half hour later, State Police Officer Henry Sinclair declared Stanley thirty sheets to the wind. They didn't even bother to handcuff Stanley before loading him into the cruiser. It was as easy and uneventful as an arrest could be, but Dave still had to issue his share of the report, so he got back in his truck and followed Henry toward the Rumford jail. They'd just turned onto Route 2 in Rumford Center when Oxford County Sheriff Bart Ames came over the radio.

"Officer needs help," Bart said, following it up with his location on Main Street in Hanover.

Dave knew Bart well enough to recognize the fear in his voice. The address was also familiar to local officers as the residence of Denny Fay, better known as Big Den for his 6'4" frame and farm strength. Denny was bipolar, a gentle giant under medicinal regulation who was prone to volcanic eruptions when off his pills. By the sound of Bart's plea, there was no doubt he was in a serious situation, and so Dave pulled a U-turn and stepped on the accelerator. In his rearview mirror, he saw Henry follow suit. When they arrived on the scene, Bart was standing at the door of his cruiser, which was serving as a protective buffer, the blue lights flashing upon the Fay family's old yellow farmhouse.

"He's inside," Bart yelled as soon as Dave and Henry were out of their vehicles. "Threatening his parents with a butcher knife."

"Have you seen the knife?" Henry asked.

"Yes, that's why I'm out here."

"Is anyone hurt?"

"I don't think so, but I don't really know. I've been out here since he threatened me."

"I'll check," Dave volunteered. "Maybe he's calmed down."

Dave opened the front door and announced, "Maine Warden Service. I'm coming in." He was three steps into the dining room when a mountain of a man confronted him. Denny had a wild look about him—enraged eyes, tousled greasy hair, and a white t-shirt drenched in sweat. Denny grunted at Dave, a warning shot before he erupted into a beastly yell. The butcher knife was nowhere in sight. Denny's weapon of choice was now a Jonsered chainsaw that he held high above his head. He squeezed the trigger and the saw's teeth nearly ripped into the ceiling as the room filled with exhaust.

A woman screamed in the back room but Denny's focus was unwavering from Dave. Beads of sweat ran down his temples as he continued to hold the roaring chainsaw overhead, his thick arms stiff as boards.

Dave was frozen in place, hands held in a surrendering position.

Denny clenched his teeth and came after him with the chainsaw running full tilt.

Dave almost wet himself. "Oh, shit!" he yelled, turning and sprinting from the house at what felt like the speed of light, the sound of the revving chainsaw step by step behind him. He dove across the hood of Bart's cruiser and popped back up with his Smith & Wesson Model 19 revolver in hand.

Denny circled the front of the vehicle. Bart was yelling at him, but Dave couldn't tell what he was saying over the chainsaw. It was a large, seventies-style saw at least a decade old that might as well have been an anvil. It would have given most men all they could handle using two hands. Not Denny. He was running it wide open, slashing the chainsaw through the air with one hand as if it were a butter knife. Dave raised his gun with full intent to fire. Out of the corner of his eye, he could see Bart was doing the same. As Dave squeezed the trigger, something clicked with Denny, and he cast the chainsaw aside. Somehow Dave managed to jam the index finger of his opposite hand under the hammer as it came down, preventing the gun from firing. Both Dave and Bart holstered their pistols as the three officers encircled Denny in a triangular formation.

"Get your cuffs out," Bart yelled to Dave.

Denny grunted and screamed as his focus swiveled amongst the officers. There was no doubt they were in for a fight. Henry and Bart were formidable men in their own right, each over six feet tall. At a rugged five feet, seven inches, and 180 pounds, Dave was no stranger to physicality, but this was way out of his weight class. Still, by pure headcount, it appeared the officers had the upper hand.

They didn't.

Dave charged into Denny's midsection in an attempt to tackle him. He might as well have run into a skidder. The next thing he knew, he was on the pavement looking up as Bart clubbed Denny over the head with a seven-cell Kel-Lite. The blow from this weighty aluminum flashlight should have brought Denny to his knees, if not knocked him out altogether. Instead, Denny barely flinched. All it really did was further incite him. Denny let out a vicious roar and turned his attention to Bart. This distraction opened the door for Henry to come at Denny from behind, getting his side-handle baton around Denny's neck in an attempt to choke him to the ground. Denny grabbed the bottom of the baton and ripped it out of Henry's hands. He flung it into the darkness as Bart shot pepper spray at his face. This action also proved futile. The three officers then charged Denny all at once. Dave lunged for the back of his legs while Henry and Bart tackled high.

The giant finally fell.

"Cuff him! Cuff him!" Bart kept yelling.

Dave found himself atop Denny's right arm. There was another man on him, and in the chaotic scramble of limbs Dave was able to get a cuff on Denny's wrist, which was so big he was only able to get one notch locked. Denny's arm shot forward, dragging Dave across the pavement. He held on to the cuffs' loose end with both hands. No matter what, he was determined not to let go. Dave was lifted into the air as Denny climbed to his feet and furiously let loose a barrage of haymakers aimed at Bart and Henry. With each punch, Dave was flung through the air like a ragdoll.

The scrum continued in this fashion for several minutes. They went to the ground, then were back up again. More punches. More wrestling. More scrambling. At one point Bart landed a second Kel-Lite blow to Denny's head, much to the same effect as the first. Soon after this, an errant punch sent Dave crashing into Henry. The two men became entangled, the force of which pulled Denny forward and caused him to trip. As Denny climbed back to his feet, Bart held the pepper spray to his eyes. This time, it worked. Falling back to his knees, Denny screamed in pain and dug his palms into his eyes. Henry knocked him flat on the ground, and the three officers piled on. Dave reached around and secured the open cuff onto Denny's left wrist.

The fight was over. All four men were lying in a heap, huffing and puffing, when a voice came over them. Dave looked up to see Stanley standing watch.

"You fellas need a hand?" Stanley asked. He was not a big man by any stretch of the imagination. About five feet, six inches tall, and thin as a cornstalk, Stanley couldn't have been more than 140 pounds soaking wet, which, considering his urine-soaked jeans, he was.

"Stanley," Dave yelled, trying not to laugh, "get back in the car!"

"Dave," Henry said as they climbed to their feet, "your shirt."

"What about it?"

"It's gone."

Sure enough, both Dave's warden top and white undershirt had been ripped off. Across his left shoulder and down onto his back was a large raspberry scrape. There was also a long rip along the inseam of his pants. He found his shirts on the pavement—what was left of them, anyway. Completely shredded, it wasn't worth trying to put them back on. And so, after they loaded Denny into the back of Henry's cruiser alongside Stanley, Dave climbed shirt-less into the front passenger seat. He turned around and held his revolver up for Denny to see.

"I'm going to keep this out on my lap," Dave said. "If you so much as wiggle, I'm going to shoot you right between the eyes."

"It's okay, Warden," Denny said. "I'm fine, I'll be good."

"You better."

They brought Denny to the Oxford County Jail in South Paris where he was already on a first-name basis with most of the staff. Upon arrival, the jailer showed them into the lockup and instructed Dave to remove the handcuffs.

"Now, wait a minute," Dave said. "I've already had one wres-tling match with him tonight. As you can see that didn't go so well for me. I've lost my shirt, my pants are nearly ripped off, and I'm all beat to hell. I think I've done my civic duty for the good people of Oxford County tonight. I got the cuffs on him, I'm not going to be the one to take them off."

"Oh, yes, you are," the jailer said. "Those are your cuffs on his wrists. Until you take them off, he's your responsibility."

Dave knew he wasn't going to win. "Denny," he said, "I'm gonna to take the cuffs off you. Listen carefully, because this is how we're going to do it. You're gonna get down on your knees and lay flat on the floor. I'm going to get on your back and unlock the cuffs. If you do anything you're not supposed to, I will shoot you—do you understand?"

"It's okay. I'll be good."

Denny did as he was told and laid on the floor with his hands locked behind his back. Dave climbed on him, standing with one foot in the middle of his back and the other on his butt. Denny's cooperation seemed too good to be true. Dave reached down and unlocked the cuffs as quick as he could.

"Denny, remember what I told you."

"I'll behave, Warden."

"Good." Dave stepped off Denny's back, stood him up, and then sat him down in a chair.

"He's all yours," Dave said to the jailer. He turned to leave.

"What about me?" Stanley asked.

"What about you?" Dave said

"If I don't behave, will you shoot me, too?"

"No, Stanley, I'll do something worse with you. I'll drop you off at your ex-wife's place."

ABOUT THE AUTHOR

Daren Worcester is a native of Hanover, Maine, and a graduate of the University of Maine. He has been published in *Backpacker* and *Down East* magazines, and he runs the website northeasthikes .com. This is his first book. Daren lives in New Hampshire with his family. Read more of his tales about the Maine Warden Service at wardenstories.com.